Group and Team Coaching

The Essential Guide

Christine Thornton

Routledge
Taylor & Francis Group

LONDON AND NEW YORK

First published 2010
by Routledge
27 Church Road, Hove, East Sussex BN3 2FA

Simultaneously published in the USA and Canada
by Routledge
711 Third Avenue, New York NY 10017 (8th Floor)

Routledge is an imprint of the Taylor & Francis Group, an Informa business

Typeset in New Century Schoolbook by
RefineCatch Limited, Bungay, Suffolk
Printed and bound in Great Britain by
TJ International Ltd, Padstow, Cornwall
Paperback cover design by Lisa Dynan

British Library Cataloguing in Publication Data
A catalogue record for this book is available from the British Library

Library of Congress Cataloging-in-Publication Data
Thornton, Christine, 1958–.
  Group & team coaching : the essential guide / Christine Thornton.
    p. cm.
  Includes bibliographical references and index.
  ISBN 978–0–415–47227–2 (hbk) – ISBN 978–0–415–47228–9 (pbk)
1. Personal coaching. 2. Teams in the workplace. I. Title. II. Title: Group and
team coaching
  BF637.P36T464 2010
  158′.35–dc22

                                    2009043133

ISBN: 978–0–415–47227–2 (hbk)
ISBN: 978–0–415–47228–9 (pbk)

Dedication

For John, who makes everything possible.

Contents

Foreword   ix
KATHERINE TULPA
Preface: what this book does   xi
Acknowledgements   xiii

Part 1   1

1 Introduction: what is group coaching?   3

Part 2   21

2 Learning, holding and exchange   23
3 Looking deeper: the secret life of groups   44
4 Eight group factors influencing learning
   and change   64

Part 3   85

5 Understanding organizations, groups and teams:
   systems thinking   87

Part 4   115

6 Team coaching   117
7 Learning group coaching   147
8 Supervision groups   164

Part 5   191

9   Strategies for tackling problem behaviour   193

10   Groups that do not work: understanding and
tackling dysfunctional patterns in group
behaviour   214

11   Managing beginnings, middles and endings:
boundaries of the group   233

Afterword   250

Part 6   251

Suggested further reading   253
Continuous professional development in the
unconscious dynamics of groups and
organizations   255
Frequently asked questions   258
References and bibliography   260
Index   269

Foreword

This book comes at a pivotal stage, as coaching emerges as a profession, rapidly becoming one of the most accepted ways to accelerate people and business performance. While coaching started off as an intervention to facilitate a manager's or leader's individual learning and development, it is now being used to drive organizational change and transformation.

At the heart of this change comes a greater understanding for coaches and those involved in driving the organization's learning agenda to be open to new perspectives in getting maximum returns from both their current and future talent. We need to look beyond conventional coaching and learning methods (i.e. 1:1 development, 'content-led' training), and tap into the *wisdom* of groups. It seems we are only at the brink of what this can generate. This book contributes to that change at many levels.

The timing is right for *Group and Team Coaching: The Essential Guide*. It is the first book to cover this growing and important area of coaching to the depth that the author, Christine Thornton, shares with us. Her experience as a coach practitioner, as well as someone well educated in the areas of group analysis and systems theory, certainly shines through here. Throughout the pages, she strikes a nice balance between what informs group coaching – the bedrock, if you will – and practical, real-world examples from her twenty-five years' experience in this field.

The coaching profession needs a book like this to appreciate where group and team coaching has evolved from (like many forms of coaching, from many disciplines) and to put a 'stake in the ground' at this stage of our evolutionary growth. It offers ideas for others to learn from, to be inspired by, and apply in practice so this very important area of coaching will advance, thereby enabling coaches, groups and organizations to reap the wider benefits.

On a broader scale, group or team coaching, as a catalyst for drawing out co-learning and collective group wisdom, can, in Christine's own words, 'foster feelings of connection and common purpose'. She notes that 'if people feel more connected to a larger, worthwhile undertaking, they work harder and stay longer because they feel good about themselves and their place in the company, and in the world'.

If we have more of that in the workplace, and in our lives, there is no doubt that this not only will produce new sources of energy for greater people and business performance, but can be the key for breaking down barriers that inhibit change. It can act as a new source for answers during challenging times, and generate new possibilities and direction – in turn, helping to transform organizations and, one can only hope, society.

Katherine Tulpa
CEO and Co-founder, Association for Coaching

Preface: what this book does

I wrote this book out of a desire to share with other group
and team coaches the group analytic insights into the 'secret
life of groups' that have enriched my practice with teams and
groups over the past twenty years.

These ideas are explored in depth in Chapters 2, 3
and 4, which are the 'must-read' section of the book. They
demystify the elemental processes of group dynamics. The
rest of the book applies these principles to the 'how to' of
group coaching in everyday situations. Though the focus is
on working with groups in organizational and business contexts, the ideas can be applied to all other kinds of coaching
group.

To our knowledge, this is the first book about group
coaching including teams. There are clearly many books
about teams, but few are written from a coaching perspective, and none from a group coaching perspective. The book's
approach, like my own, is fundamentally pluralistic, deriving
value from the ideas of different, even apparently contradictory, traditions.

The book's core aim is itself paradoxical: to explain
complex ideas about group dynamics in terms clear and simple enough to provide a tool of value to coaches and allied
professionals. It:

- explores the question 'what is group coaching?'
- explains the fundamentals of group dynamics and the
  interpersonal processes underpinning group coaching
- offers practical guidance about 'how to do group coaching
  in organizations'.

Coaching professionals typically seek new insight in a book like this, information to illuminate practice, and practical guidance to be weighed against experience. Using the principles described in the book requires the coach to think rigorously about the purpose, context and membership of each group with whom s/he works; doing so enables us to craft, with each group, appropriate methodologies, depth, and frankness of engagement.

Business professionals might use the book a little differently. Organizations use a wide range of group interventions with the intention of achieving positive change, often with little guidance about the merits of particular approaches in particular circumstances. In 1996 a classic study found that only 30% of organizational change programmes succeed, a finding confirmed by many other studies over subsequent years.[1] This book sheds light on why this might be, and offers data relevant to the business professional choosing between competing group coaching proposals.

The book in a nutshell

The book has six parts. The first part tackles the question 'what is group coaching?', and explores the differences between groups and teams. Part 2 connects group theory, which may be quite new even to the experienced coach, to group and team coaching. Part 3 introduces systems theory as a way of thinking about whole organizations. Part 4 reviews and provides advice in three main areas of group coaching: teams, learning groups and supervision groups. Part 5 covers specific issues and problems that arise in working with groups, offering practical strategies for tackling these, and for setting things up well from the start. Part 6 offers information about further resources.

Finally, this is a book that must be tested against experience, so that the insights it offers can inform practice. Please read it all in the light of your own experiences in groups.

Christine Thornton
March 2010

Acknowledgements

I am profoundly grateful to my partners in research, whose generous input is a foundation of the book: Amanda Bowens, Claudia Demuth, Hilary Fellows, Heather Williams and Tina Waterman-Roberts.

The following people made innumerable valuable responses and suggestions that have improved what you now read. They have been the group that fostered the development of the book: any remaining flaws are my responsibility and not theirs. Linda Aspey, Nick Barwick, Linda Bennett, Martin Bhurruth, Dick Blackwell, Sally Britton, Halina Brunning, Kate Buller, Alison Dale, William Erb, Irene MacWilliam, Morris Nitsun, Cynthia Rogers, Fiona Scrase, Meg Sharpe, Gill Smith and Katherine Tulpa, and the series editors, Averil Leimon, Gladeana MacMahon and Stephen Palmer. Thanks too to Joanna Forshaw and Dawn Harris, my patient and helpful editors at Routledge, and Judith Frank for invaluable help with the index.

I am grateful to my clients, colleagues and supervisees for our work together, which is reflected in the vignettes and in the ideas that the book presents.

Thanks to Jacki Nicholas for help on group telephone coaching, and to Christina Bachini, Kate Greenwood, Adrian Goodall, Mandy Gutsell, Andie Heming, Michelle McCue, Polly McDonald, Jonathan Wilson and all other AC members who generously shared ideas and information, whether or not I have been able to include them in the final cut.

Part 1

Introduction: what is group coaching?

This chapter

This chapter discusses what group coaching is, and reviews its uses. It explains what the rest of the book is about, and how it might be used.

Groups

Groups are everywhere. We live in small groups, from family to friends to work group, with untold impact on the quality of our lives.

Groups are powerful. They have great positive potential, and yet 'bad' group experiences are (rightly) feared (see Chapters 3 and 4). To work effectively with groups, we must harness their power to achieve change, while minimizing destructive elements. At their best, groups offer a profound encounter

This chapter contains:
- This chapter
- Groups
- Group coaching in organizations
- Underlying group principles
- Advantages of group coaching
- The need for standards for group coaching
- What is group coaching?
- When is a group a team?
- What every coach needs to know
- How the book came about, and how you might use it
- Group analysis: the fundamental dynamics of group life
- Systems thinking: the fundamental dynamics of organizational life
- The vignettes in the book are real examples
- What does the book contain?

with others that promotes collaboration, creative challenge and adaptation.

Groups are fundamental. Being in and learning to cooperate effectively within groups, is the root not only of business success, but of all our achievements as a species. Even a genius builds on the discoveries of those who have gone before – in the words of Newton, on the shoulders of giants. As a species our collective genius is to adapt, and we do so by learning from one another. For humans, 'the relationship precedes the individual'.[2] The individual develops a sense of self through interaction with others, and all our learning, from the earliest moments of life, occurs in a relational context. See 'Learning, holding and exchange' in Chapter 2.

Group coaching in organizations

Every company is a group – sometimes a very large one – organized by being broken down into smaller groups. In effective coaching groups, learning is multiplied as people learn from each other's dilemmas as well as their own. Over time, these experiences can develop flexibility and interpersonal skills to a high degree. In this way groups can make a tangible contribution to business advantage, but equally importantly, influence the intangibles that underlie long-term business health and prosperity.

Put simply, if people feel more connected to a larger, worthwhile undertaking, they work harder and stay longer because they feel good about themselves and their place in the company, and in the world. All executive coaching is to some degree a bridging process, helping the individual make sense of, and work effectively in, the context of their organization. Better than any other kind of intervention, well-run groups can foster feelings of connection and common purpose.

Groups are essential to the development of effective leadership and collaboration skills. New advances in neuroscience persuaded Daniel Goleman to extend his concept of emotional intelligence to *social intelligence*, a more relationally based understanding of the interpersonal competencies needed to inspire others to be effective.[3] Groups are by far the most effective method for developing these competencies.

In difficult economic times, successful companies understand that planning long term, and keeping staff well motivated and involved in solving business problems, is critical. We have all heard of 'groupthink', the reductive process through which group members systematically exclude information needed to make better quality decisions when faced with challenges (see 'Groups and decision-making' in Chapter 5). Properly led groups, on the contrary, can help people face hard realities together, fostering resolve and generating creative, realistic solutions to business challenges. Groups can help individuals overcome stress and other 'knee-jerk' responses to threat or change, and so work productively once again. In troubled economic waters, this may be the difference between sinking and swimming.

Group coaching includes two broad areas: team coaching, and coaching learning groups, which are groups that have come together for the purpose of learning. A global survey of group coaching conducted in 2008[4] identified that around 60% of group coaching was targeted on intact teams, and around 40% on coaching groups of individuals from different organizations.[5] The group coach is always working with one of these. This is a simplification, but it is a useful one for the practitioner. The differences between teams and learning groups are discussed further in 'When is a group a team?' below.

Underlying group principles

Given all this, our general ignorance of the dynamics and principles of group life, at least at a conscious level, is remarkable. It is perhaps only sustainable because it is balanced by a *non-conscious* shared 'knowing' about group life. That is observable in every gathering, and includes a commonly felt sense that people learn in groups.

To use this to advantage in business coaching, we must grasp more fully the group processes that can underpin, or undermine, learning and change. We must engage with the non-conscious as well as the rational. If we understand better the non-rational obstacles that overturn our carefully laid plans, we are better placed to overcome them; if we understand how group processes can rally people around a shared goal, people in our organizations will flourish and work with ingenuity.

This book articulates these underlying group principles. It illustrates how they apply to group coaching in a business context. In all groups we can attend to the fundamentals that encourage people to engage with and learn from each other.

There are important differences between groups, factors such as organizational context, size, longevity, physical proximity and individual capacities, which promote and/or limit the group's capacity for learning. The art and science of group coaching is balancing a realistic assessment of the state of affairs and the people in it, including the coach, with a sense of the transformational potential of the group situation.

Advantages of group coaching

Groups can be highly time- and cost-efficient for organizations. They can also be highly inefficient, for example if in the grip of 'groupthink' (see Chapter 5). A group coach works with several people simultaneously *and* helps them harness their power to help each other. In a challenging business environment, coming together to reflect on pressing problems can generate ideas tested and refined to a robust degree of usability, provided the group coach enables the team to engage honestly with the real challenges. The need to develop skilful group discussion has rarely been more pressing.

The opportunities for learning are multiplied by the number of different individuals in the coaching relationship,[6] since everyone brings different skills and experience to the table. Some of the factors that enhance learning in a group context are:

- the availability of role models
- the amplification of learning responses in a group setting

- the power of peer pressure
- the pressure to engage with and understand business realities, including unpalatable ones
- the opportunity to identify with something larger than ourselves and feel part of a greater endeavour
- the ability of peers to correct and challenge each other in a direct and natural way
- the strengthening of identification with the company and its goals and values
- the development of flexibility through direct and repeated contact with others' different views and approaches
- learning to live more comfortably with uncertainty and chaos, since group experience is never predictable.

In addition to the benefits of peer coaching and learning through peer exchange,[7] group coaching helps teams build collaboration and understand more fully each other's styles, strengths and weaknesses. In all groups there are personal learning opportunities, through quietly comparing ourselves with others, to understand more fully our own strengths and weaknesses. In a coaching group this process is greatly enhanced, because individual learning is an explicit goal and members can voice these thoughts, and test them against the perceptions of others.

Disadvantages to group coaching arise where groups are too large for individual attention to be given, where contribution levels vary too much (i.e. some members dominant, some very quiet), and in cultures and situations where loss of face is very important, inhibiting exchange. Most of these disadvantages can be addressed by careful design of the group, as regards size, composition, methodology and coach skill set.[8]

Indeed, for a group to be a coaching group (as opposed to, say, a training course or a lecture), it must be small enough that attention can be paid to individual learning needs. It is not that *learning* cannot take place in larger groups. It is that *coaching* is fundamentally addressed to individual learning, whether in a one-to-one or a group context. Even team coaching, where learning goals are shared, relies on individuals learning and changing their behaviour.

The need for standards for group coaching

At the time of writing, the boundaries of group coaching are less than clear. For instance, many coaches do not clearly differentiate intact teams from other kinds of group. This book offers a definition of group coaching and the standards that should be applied to doing it, hoping to stimulate a broader discussion in the profession as a whole. Lewin, a 'founding father', commented that in group dynamics, theory and practice are closely interlinked:[9] practitioners together must address these questions.

The world of coaching is a broad church, with a plurality of orientations and skill sets. It is helpful to be clear and rigorous about the conditions and standards that enable a group to engage in mutual coaching, but unhelpful to be very prescriptive about what activities might be included. The question of standards is important, because group coaching carries a higher risk than individual coaching of being diluted through mislabelling. For example, getting a training group involved in discussion is not group coaching, nor is a one-hour telephone teleclass for 25 strangers. Individual learning can occur in either of these, but sustained attention to individual development cannot.

In order to be coaching, there must be attention to the learning needs of the individuals in the group, only possible in smaller groups; the group must also meet over time so that learning can be incrementally built upon, fine-tuned and consolidated. As well as size and longevity of the group, the nature of the relationships is important. A coaching group has to be small enough for all participants to be active learners *through interaction with each other*. It is here that the unique benefits of group coaching can be reaped.

To achieve the highest possible standards of group practice across the profession, we also have to clarify what outcomes group coaching can offer. In Chapters 6, 7 and 8 we discuss some likely outcomes in coaching teams and learning groups. More importantly, the book offers some principles that can be applied to all group coaching contexts by thoughtful practitioners. Whatever their modality, group coaches should be conversant with the dynamics of group life. And in fact, group coaches tend to be drawn from among more experienced coaches.[10]

The book therefore argues for an inclusive definition of group coaching as regards styles and processes, combined with a rigorous definition as regards issues affecting standards of practice, such as numbers and longevity.

What is group coaching?

A coaching group is:

> a small group of people meeting together in active participation on several occasions, for the purpose of learning, including developing new capacities and skills. Participants learn through exchange and interaction with each other.

Rather than one specific method, group coaching is the application of principles of group dynamics to a variety of methods, in order to increase the effectiveness and reach of the results. The interaction between participants is a key element.

Group coaching takes place in small groups, that is, groups of up to ten people in team coaching (where the learning objectives are shared), and rather fewer in learning group coaching (where the objectives are individual). The typical size of an action learning set, for example, is six. (See 'Learning group coaching versus team coaching' in Chapter 7.) Groups larger than ten are unlikely to offer enough attention to individual learning needs.[11]

Experience suggests that the ideal face-to-face size is around five to eight – large enough for a good range of experiences and views, and for individuals' moment-to-moment intensity of involvement to vary, and small enough that all members feel some impetus to participate. On the telephone, where participants as well as coach must work harder to interpret aural clues, the most effective size is smaller still.

In a smaller group than this, the experience is less rich for participants, and there is pressure on the coach to adopt a dual role of both coaching and participating. In a larger one, there is not enough time for everyone to participate actively and time limits attention to individual learning needs. If an intact team is larger than this, it may be worth subdividing it for the purposes of coaching, while coming together for some whole-team activities.

As groups get larger, participants move to a more receptive style of learning, as in a lecture, where we receive information and opinion and quietly evaluate it. There is a brief discussion of some creative methods for working with larger groups in Chapter 5.

In larger groups we are more likely to tune out, which is why training groups are routinely broken into smaller units for active tasks. Tuning out is also more likely in telephone groups, where visual communication signals are not available, and e-groups, where, unlike leaving the lecture hall, we can vote with our (virtual) feet without anyone necessarily noticing.

Coaching does not happen in one meeting. All coaching relationships, individual or group, imply some longevity of engagement – the learning takes place over time, and so involves meeting on a number of occasions, with the opportunity to sustain and build on previous learning through repeated reflection. What is distinctive about group coaching is that the relationship is multiple. Each member of the group can relate to the coach, to each other member and to the group as a whole, with the added learning choices and possibilities implied.

Group coaching:

- requires active interaction between participants
- requires a small group (3–10)
- takes place over time
- has a learning focus directed by the participants, not the coach
- involves some face-to-face engagement
- learning groups require individual goals, teams a common goal.

Coaching requires that the learner be involved in setting the learning objectives. A training course with fixed content is not a coaching group, though many group principles still apply, particularly those about starting and ending well, and encouraging transfer of learning. (See Chapter 11.) A training or management development programme, with repeated meetings over time, can be designed to incorporate group coaching sessions, and these can maximize the impact of what is learned.

The fifth point in the box, the need for face-to-face engagement, is perhaps the most controversial. For further discussion of telephone and distance coaching, see 'Coaching virtual teams' in Chapter 6 and 'Group telephone coaching' in Chapter 7.

When is a group a team?

Slightly more than half of group coaching assignments are directed to coaching intact teams. The most fundamental question about any group coaching assignment is: is this a learning group, or is it a team?

All teams are groups,[12] but not all groups are teams. A team has an explicit shared purpose and/or task, usually in a broader organizational context. It usually exists before and after the coaching intervention, with communication patterns and a network of relationships already established.

Teams and learning groups have different kinds of objectives. In team coaching, common learning goals are important; this does not preclude individual feedback and learning, indeed it requires it. The individual learning is however in the service of the team achieving its shared purpose more effectively.

Where group participants are not members of one intact team, but have come together as relative strangers for the purpose of individual learning, the coach is instead dealing with a learning group. The group's goal is the self-directed learning of its individual members; the variety of goals, together with the commitment to aid each other's learning, results in a deep, cross-fertilizing learning experience. This richness of learning arises from the fact that learners set and work actively on *different* learning goals, and does not preclude sharing profound insights, nor the significant refining of members' interpersonal and collaborative skills; in fact, in a successful learning group, these outcomes are inevitable.

The team/learning group distinction is not a philosophical one, but geared unashamedly to the needs of the

---

Learning groups

The 'learning group' is a group brought together for the purposes of learning. The coach usually works with the group from the outset, and is present at all meetings.[13] Members are not close colleagues, nor in the same team, nor are they in competition in the normal course of working. They may work for different organizations. Examples of this kind of coaching group are the action learning set, the Balint group, the reflective practice group, the professional development group, and the supervision group.

Teams

From the coach's point of view, a team is a work group with shared goals or tasks, usually in a broader organizational context. The team is varied by size, longevity, diversity, stability, and boundaries of membership and purpose, all of which affect how the group coach can work (see Chapter 7). New kinds of team structure, teams with fluid, single-task-focused or time-limited boundaries, and the possibility for truly global teams created by advances in communication technology make team coaching highly complex. We cannot assume stable membership or geographical propinquity; there are new uncertainties, and, especially in cross-cultural teams, broad possibilities for miscommunication.

practitioner. It is critical in designing effective learning interventions. To add another layer of complexity, if we look at the organizational level, learning groups are often used by larger companies as a tool for wider organizational change. They seed culture change across a company, by developing individuals in strategic positions in *different* teams.

What every coach needs to know

All executive coaching, group or individual, takes place in an organizational context. The diagram overleaf sets out the context of individual coaching.

The coach working with the individual-in-the-organization must have knowledge in at least three fields: psychological literacy to understand the client, good inter-personal skills to facilitate the learning process, and a grasp of organizational life that enables a joint understanding to develop, with the client, of the work context.

The effective group coach needs all these, plus knowledge of a fourth field, group dynamics. See 'Developing the capacity to hold a group', 'Holding as time goes on' and 'What enables the group coach to hold a group effectively?' in Chapter 2, and 'The roles of the group coach' in Chapter 4.

How the book came about and how you might use it

I have been a professional working with groups for twenty-five years. In my work, I became fascinated by the processes through which individuals learn in groups, and eighteen years ago began the process of training as a group analyst. As I began to conduct analytic therapy groups alongside my work with organizations, I became excited by the encounter with group analytic theory. It seemed to me that what I was learning could account for much that I had observed in all kinds of groups. (I was already convinced of the value of systemic and analytic views of whole organizations and individual behaviour.) I became convinced, through my experiences in groups, of the fundamental similarities in the

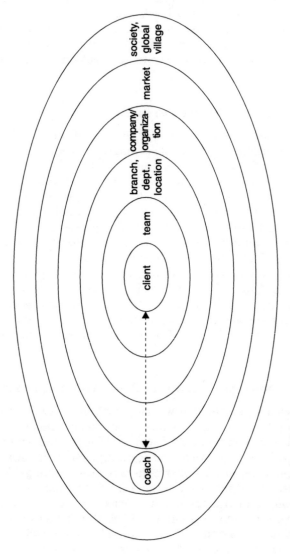

The context of coaching

processes through which individuals in groups learn and change,[14] irrespective of the nature or the focus of the group.

It is these processes, and how they play out in groups, that form the conceptual core of the book. This makes it vital to read Chapters 2, 3 and 4 thoroughly. These chapters articulate the principles that inform the rest of the book, and to miss them is to overlook core principles that can be applied to all kinds of groups, in contexts as various as team development, professional development, supervision, learning groups and training.

Just as the diagram opposite moves from the individual through the team to the broader organization and beyond, the conceptual chapters move from the learning processes that inform individual development, to how these play out in groups, to the interpersonal processes in groups. Chapter 3 deals with core group analytic concepts, and Chapter 4 with further important factors uncovered by various researchers, including my own action research (2006–2008) into what aspects of group life promote confidence and competence. Digesting the material from these three chapters can give group coaches a framework for understanding how to develop context-specific interventions.

While research has demonstrated a link between these interpersonal learning processes and an organization's ability to learn,[15] a further link is needed between the inter-action of the group (quite properly the focus of the group coach and the team coach) and the organizational context that both influences and is influenced by what happens there. The team coach cannot ignore this. (Nor can the individual coach.) Systems theory, modulated through complexity and chaos theory, is this link, offering a means of understanding wholes and the relationships between parts. Chapter 5 offers a whistle-stop tour of systems thinking, an overview of these ways of understanding organizations. It also introduces some research into group decision-making, and techniques that rely on the self-organizing principle of emergence for use with larger groups. One of the central tenets of group analysis is the validity of differing, even contradictory views in forming a fuller picture. Coaches concerned with the value of diversity in organizations will understand this.

All the foregoing emphasizes the importance of theory to practice, and, in a young profession like coaching, a literature based on practice and research is necessarily in its infancy. This is especially true of group coaching, and so theory must be applied from 'allied trades'. The theory described in this book is drawn mainly from the two fields mentioned above, with some support from the psychological disciplines. The underlying principles of group life are largely derived from *group analysis*. The underlying understanding of organizational life, within which groups operate, is derived from *systems theory*. The two disciplines are linked by common roots in a new paradigm in the sciences and social sciences, and are widely used in organizational consultation.

Group analysis: the fundamental dynamics of group life

Group analysis is an internationally established discipline with seventy years' practice-based theoretical literature: 'the instrument of choice for the study of the dynamics of the group' and 'a science in which psychology and sociology meet'.[16] It articulates fundamental processes that can be observed in all groups, and pays particular attention to the relationship between each individual in the group and the group as a whole.

The balancing of attention between individual and group functioning is highly relevant to coaching groups, and particularly to teams, where high functioning requires that the relationship between the individual members and the group as a whole be in optimal balance. In demanding modern business environments, teams no longer have the luxury of performing at less than their best because they are unable to collaborate. The achievement of team goals (and their continual re-definition in many industries) requires that the interpersonal obstacles to successful cooperation be minimized.

Systems thinking: the fundamental dynamics of organizational life

In order to understand a team or group within an organization, we must understand something of the business context. New science has taught us that the complexity and inter-relatedness of all contexts is greater than we ever dreamed of. Over the past half century, discoveries in many sciences have converged. New understandings from biology, neuroscience, mathematics and physics meet discoveries in psychology, sociology and ecology as part of a broader paradigm shift[17] emphasizing the complex interconnectedness of the universe. Systems theory, incorporating chaos and complexity theory, has articulated how these understandings apply in the organizational field. These ideas provide the book's framework for understanding organizations.

The vignettes in the book are real examples

Throughout the book, vignettes illustrate the concepts described and relate them to group coaching situations. These stories are drawn from my own coaching experiences, and those of colleagues and supervisees, with details changed to safeguard anonymity.

What does the book contain?

Part 1

This introductory chapter constitutes Part 1.

Part 2

The second, third and fourth chapters are the conceptual core of the book, articulating principles of group life. Chapter 2 explores the relational basis of the human learning process, and its application to group coaching. Chapter 3 articulates nine core group processes. Chapter 4 explores eight factors affecting how we learn in groups, and summarizes the roles of the group coach and the team coach.

Part 3

Part 3, which consists of Chapter 5, addresses the organiza-tional context of group coaching, and introduces systems theory as a way of understanding how coach and team, or coach and group, are located and related in the organization. For the business leader, the question of how two or several teams interact, how the best decisions are made, or what is communicated informally across the company can be more pressing than the performance of a particular team, and these areas are touched upon, as is decision-making research; there is also a review of methods of working with larger groups.

Part 4

Part 4 reviews current applications of group coaching, to help the practitioner design successful interventions. Chapter 6 focuses on team coaching, proposing a pragmatic approach responsive to the client's desired objectives and starting point, and offers guidelines for choosing among the many tools available to the team coach. It opens a discuss-ion of challenging team dynamics that is continued in Chapter 10. Chapter 7 outlines four kinds of learning group. Chapter 8 is concerned with the dynamics of a particular kind of learning group, supervision groups, and with the supervision of group coaching.

Part 5

Part 5 offers practical guidance on issues that commonly arise in our work with groups and teams. Chapter 9 focuses on how to tackle individuals' behaviour in groups, and how to capitalize on it for team learning; Chapter 10 is concerned with teams and groups that do not work; Chapter 11 looks at the impact of time (beginning, middle and end), and at the 'system administration' (attention to the total environment) of group coaching.

Part 6

This brief resource section brings together suggested further reading, a list of some institutions that offer experiential training in working with the unconscious dynamics of groups and/or organizations, and a frequently asked questions section that sits alongside the index and contents pages as a way to navigate the book. The references and the index can be found at the end of this section.

Part 2

Concepts discussed in Part 2		
Chapter 2: Learning, holding and exchange	**Chapter 3: Looking deeper: the secret life of groups**	**Chapter 4: Eight group factors influencing learning and change**
Two fundamentals	*Nine group processes*	*Eight group factors*
Implicit knowing	Group matrix	Connectedness and belonging
Projection	Communication	Interpersonal learning
Transference	Translation	
Holding	Mirroring	Competition, envy and admiration
Exchange	Exchange	Idealization and emulation
	Resonance	Practising courage
	Condenser phenomena	Witnessing and being witnessed
	Location	Encouragement
	The reflection process	Group performance coaching

Part 2 (Chapters 2, 3 and 4) is the conceptual core of the book. It sets out the interpersonal processes underpinning all learning and cooperation. It describes complex processes as simply as possible, to make a useful body of theory, drawn from psychological and social sciences, available to a wider audience. Part 2 is concerned with how groups help people learn and develop confidence.

2

Learning, holding and exchange

Part 2's opening page (p. 21) shows how this chapter links to group themes overall.

Two fundamentals
Implicit knowing
Projection
Transference
Holding
Exchange

This chapter contains:
- This chapter
- The antiquity of groups
- 'Implicit knowing'
- Projection
- Transference
- The two fundamentals of all coaching: holding and exchange
- Holding
- Learning, holding and exchange
- The development of thinking and obstacles to learning
- Learning is multi-sensory and grounded in emotional relationship
- Holding and exchange in groups
- Developing the capacity to hold a group
- Holding a group
- Holding difficult feelings: using all the information about work
- Holding as time goes on
- What enables the group coach to hold a group effectively?
- Exchange
- Conventionalized exchange in action learning sets and team coaching
- Final remarks about exchange

This chapter

This chapter sets out some essential concepts. It opens with a discussion of 'implicit knowing', 'projection', and 'transference', which are central to communication processes and to emotional and social intelligence. It discusses learning, focusing on a pair of ideas: 'holding' – establishing a sense of safety – and 'exchange' – enabling the encounter with something new. These are fundamental to all learning, and so to all coaching, and are discussed in relation to group coaching.

The antiquity of groups

The processes through which groups promote individual learning and change are widely relied upon, but little comprehended. For many people, why and how groups help people to learn is something of a mystery.

'The relationship precedes the individual',[18] and we can speculate that the power of group learning has its origin in *our* origin as creatures who survived by cooperating in a group. Many theoreticians provide evidence for the unavoidably social context of learning.[19] Groups were our original element, and being in a well-functioning group can give a profound feeling of security and well-being. Conversely, we greatly fear bad group experiences. Most of our responses in groups are automatic, below the conscious level most of the time. This is because we are well adapted to understand non-conscious, non-verbal communication in groups. Recent neuroscientific discoveries suggest that our brains are actually constructed to respond to others, and join up with the work of Daniel Goleman, who has recently extended his concept of 'emotional intelligence' to 'social intelligence'.[20] Goleman argues that this ability to influence others' mood and experience is essential to outstanding leaders.

'Implicit knowing'

Daniel Stern, whose work blends developmental psychology with psychoanalytic insights, speaks of 'implicit knowing' – our 'non-symbolic, nonverbal, procedural awarenesses':

> we feel it in our body and sense it in our mind, together. You can also grasp what a group is experiencing. Our nervous systems are constructed to be captured by the nervous systems of others . . . we resonate with and participate in their experiences, and they in ours.[21]

Groups are particularly good at bringing these unnoticed aspects of knowledge into the conscious realm, because the multiple perspectives of the individual members 'amplify' the communication and act as a reality check on each other.

For this reason, in the interpersonal arena, groups score heavily over every other kind of professional development. While individual coaching offers an opportunity for effective feedback from one other person, group coaching offers the client a far wider range of perceptions and responses. As an arena for interpersonal learning and developing interpersonal skills, properly run groups cannot be equalled.

Projection

In psychological writing, projection is a defence mechanism in which we attribute parts of ourselves to others. These parts are disowned characteristics, often parts of ourselves that we do not like and prefer not to be aware of. The process is unconscious, so we are not aware that the projected characteristic is our own.

Examples of projection

- I do not like to think of myself as arrogant, so deny my arrogance and regard another person as arrogant
- I am unfaithful, and I suppress my guilt while feeling worried about whether my partner is faithful
- I do not like myself and so imagine that other people do not like me.

For me, the other person then carries my disowned arrogance, unfaithfulness or disliking. Sometimes the person I project onto shares some of my disowned characteristic, and may project theirs on me, so that we are mutually critical of the same characteristics. In group analytic thinking this is called 'negative mirroring' (see Chapter 3).

Not everything we project is negative: we can project positive aspects of ourselves, for example regarding the group coach, or a senior colleague, as having all the expertise in the world, while we 'know nothing'. Whether its content is positive or negative, projection cuts us off from awareness of our whole selves.

Projection can be seen as a more extreme form of an everyday psychological process. When communicating, we all the time compare ourselves and understand each other through innumerable small identifications and distinctions. Our perceptions are always influenced, and sometimes distorted, by our previous experiences: we never have 20:20 psychological vision.

Transference

Transference is a particular form of projection. It is a pattern of relating to others in the present, influenced by projections resulting from patterns in past relationships. It is a specific misinterpretation of relationship, which through repetition becomes self-fulfilling in the present. Strong feelings in the here and now are related to my past experiences. The past comes alive in the present, triggered by something happening in a relationship now. The process occurs below consciousness, in a way analogous to how smells can evoke strong memories.

Examples of transference

- I have the strongest sense at this moment that my boss is just like my beloved father
- I experience the same emotions towards a team colleague that I felt towards my brother, with whom I competed
- My current work situation feels just like a traumatic period at school in my teenage years.

My behaviour towards the people who are the objects of my transference is likely to provoke behaviour in them that 'matches' my transference, entrenching my belief.

These two concepts, projection and transference, are connected with 'mirroring' in groups, which is discussed in Chapter 3. It is worth highlighting that because we evaluate all new experience on the basis of prior experience, minor projective and transference reactions are normal and to be found everywhere – for instance when we feel warm or cool towards someone new, or say 'you are just like my friend Jane'.

The clue that problematic transference may be present is in how intense and how apposite the feeling is: when the emotional response is disproportionate and/or inappropriate to present reality, it is likely to be transference.

In a coaching group, the first priority is to help people recover their grip on present reality, and the group's feedback is often the most effective route. Minor projective misunderstandings are resolved in groups all the time, sometimes without ever being spoken aloud, as people 'get to know each other better'. More persistent misunderstandings, which affect individual or group functioning, require the group coach to take a more active stance.

The two fundamentals of all coaching: holding and exchange

All coaching is founded in a developmental relationship blending enough safety in the relationship to enable an encounter with new information, which Gregory Bateson has defined as 'news of difference'.[22] Holding is establishing a sense of safety in the relationship, which enables the individual's encounter with something new. That encounter is called 'exchange'.

Holding

The core skill in all coaching, as in all relationships supporting development, is *holding*:[23] the capacity to enable clients to feel safe enough to learn. The term 'holding' derives from Donald Winnicott's work on the mother–baby relationship, the first learning relationship. Holding means 'not only the actual physical holding of the infant, but also the total environmental provision'. 'Holding' allows the baby to develop as a true self, '*alone . . . in the presence of mother*'.[24] If the holding is good enough, exchange can happen.

Closely allied to holding is the concept 'containing'.[25] The difference between the two is largely a matter of focus. Both are theories about development in the very early stages of life: holding dwells more on the total experience, whereas containing focuses more on the parts – the metabolizing of frustration or discomforting experiences, to produce thought. In a group context, both ideas are close to the 'group matrix' (see Chapter 3), the group as secure ground 'holding' the individual and making her/his experience 'containable'.[26] In supervision too, the literature places holding and containing at the centre of successful supervisory relationships (Chapter 8).

Vignette: Holding reflective space in a career

Galvin had worked with the same client, Julia, over a period of seventeen years. The work was not continuous, but in four or five spells when Julia had contacted Galvin to help her with a new or changing role, Julia finally becoming a director. What tied all the assignments together was a focus on understanding Julia's current role and its requirements, and the quality of their relationship in which Julia felt accepted and understood. Julia commented that she always felt 'in completely safe hands' with Galvin, 'and that gives me free rein'.

Coaches are rightly nervous of creating dependency in their clients, and yet paradoxically a kind of *temporary* dependence is at the heart of all our work: the capacity to engender in the client a sense of enough safety, so that s/he can take in and learn from a new experience, including receiving difficult feedback. This may be for a few sessions or, as in the example, over a number of years.

Learning, holding and exchange

Why does learning require this psychological context? It is hard-wired, related to the underlying processes through which we learn. Learning occurs through balancing of security and risk. Both are necessary, from our earliest youth.

As babies and young children, if things go right for us, we explore the world from the secure base of someone who cares for us. We feel secure enough to encounter new things and new experiences, some of which are unsettling or even frightening, as well as intriguing. We need to know that we can beat a retreat to a safe pair of arms for comfort if the new experiences become overwhelming. As time goes on, through repetition we are able to tolerate the new experience more readily, and to bear different risks and greater intervals between seeking safety. In other words, we develop confidence.

Throughout life, in order to learn, we must encounter something new, something different to our previous experience, that momentarily disorients us. We then put it side by side with previous experience to see how it fits into our world, or how our world needs to be remade to accommodate this new information.[27] This *exchange*, together with the security of holding, is at the root of all coaching relationships, both individual and group. It remains easier to learn when we feel fundamentally secure and valued.

The development of thinking and obstacles to learning

Why is it sometimes so difficult to learn? Or to remember what we have learned in the past? To examine the roots of this, we must dig deep. Wilfred Bion's theory of how thinking develops offers insight into the difficulties of learning. He proposes that thinking develops as a means to link thoughts. Thoughts come first. When the baby expects to be fed and is fed, Bion calls the experience a conception: expectation matches experience. When the baby expects to be fed and is not fed, expectation does not match experience, and results in frustration. If the baby can tolerate the frustration, it becomes a thought. The baby can retain the *idea* of being fed, even while not being fed. If the baby cannot tolerate the frustration, and must get rid of it,[28] thought does not arise, and the development of thinking is disrupted. This is what happens when the holding is not 'good enough'. Every frustration has the potential to produce either a thought or a refusal to tolerate it which disrupts the capacity to think.[29]

Thought is therefore born from an experience of frustration or disorientation, and thinking develops to link up thoughts. The process of thinking arises from linking many experiences of thought. There is a stage of frustration in all learning, a disjunction or not-knowing that can be tolerated and lead to a new realization; or the opportunity to learn can be refused. This is the central paradox of learning, noted by social scientists from Lewin onwards.[30] We all both want to learn and resist learning. Coaches ignore this reality at their peril.

Chris Argyris, who has devoted more than forty years to studying the ways in which individuals in organizations evade learning, describes the defensive routines through which these processes are played out in organizational life. His work is described further in 'When working with conflicting expectations' in Chapter 6 and in Chapter 10.

Learning is multi-sensory and grounded in emotional relationship

Learning is always an intellectual *and* an emotional experience[31] at least; in infancy, it is an amalgamated experience which takes in a range of senses and dynamics – movement, sound, sight, smell – inextricably connected to the experience of learning.[32]

Consider a typical game played between carers and babies involving chanting, touch, finger movement, eye contact and shifts in facial expressions, shifts in intonation and a crescendo of experience that culminates in tickling under the arm, usually followed by giggles as the decrescendo occurs:

> Round and round the garden
> Like a teddy bear
> One step – two step
> And *tickly* under there!

The infant is learning in several sensory modalities at once, in the context of a (warm) relationship with another person whom (s/he is discovering through the pattern variations in the game) s/he can influence, but cannot directly control. Babies learn in the context of relationship, and they learn to attune emotionally *before* they learn to communicate verbally.[33]

The baby's learning is inextricably bound to the full sensory array of that original experience. Cognition, when it arrives, always takes place in a context of emotion and relies on multimodal memories of experience: the baby connects experiences, to create patterns that make sense of the experience. This too is hard-wired: we are creatures who understand by connecting, making patterns.[34]

All coaches have worked with clients who understood intellectually why they were stuck, but were nevertheless unable to put change into practice until they had more fully explored the emotional blocks to progress. True learning must involve head, heart and gut, and by bringing what was previously unconsidered into the light of day, we increase the client's chances of consciously integrating the information coming from all three.

Holding and exchange in groups

Just as they are essential to individual learning, holding and exchange are also the foundation of effective learning in groups. Where there is adequate holding, the group begins to find an appropriate level of mutual challenge (exchange). This will usually start small, as, like the exploring toddler, we take small risks. When those risks pay off, we gain confidence to take bigger ones. Over time the greater safety of a group enables greater and greater risk.

Effective group coaching
- Keeping the group safe enough to enable learning
- Encouraging curiosity and exchange of views.

There is therefore a familiar paradox at the heart of working with groups: most of us can remember a time when we felt safe enough to take a risk. If there is not sufficient safety, group members cannot risk truly learning. Some kinds of behaviour among members can make a group feel less safe, and may need active engagement from the group coach. See 'Limiting scapegoating and other destructive behaviour' in Chapter 4 and Chapter 9.

Developing the capacity to hold a group

Many coaches have an innate capacity to work with groups, but all need to deepen and develop that capacity to coach groups effectively. It is curious that while we now devote considerable energy to developing our capacities and competence as individual coaches, the same rigour is rarely applied to learning how to work with groups.

Real skill cannot be learned from a book in either arena, since so much of the capacity operates at a non-conscious level. It must be learned experientially. Only by being and learning in groups ourselves, including studying that experience, can we learn to make groups safe places for others to learn. At the end of the book is a list of organizations providing this kind of experiential learning.

A book *can* however describe what is involved, so that we can recognize it when we see it, and through greater understanding begin to learn what we need to learn.

Holding a group

Effective coaches have the capacity to hold their clients; effective group coaches must have something more. They must have the ability to hold a group of clients simultaneously, containing more difficult feelings and stronger projections than with one person. For a team, or other group within a single organization, they also have to hold the impact of that broader system on the group they are working with – all the norms and expectations that organization members carry with them, many of them not conscious. See further Chapter 5.

'Holding' is the fundamental condition of all functional groups. Here is a group member's description of what being 'held' in a new group feels like:

> The way you managed the group at the beginning which meant that the boundaries were clear . . . the closest analogy I can think of is like a baby in its mother's arms – a baby can move around but it still knows that its mother is protecting it – so in a way you are protecting a group from going all over the place.

So what is good 'holding' in a coaching group? Clearly at the outset of the group, firm boundaries and a kindly welcome are important, particularly for the wariest members. The demeanour of the coach early on is critical; people coming to something new need to know that they are in a 'safe pair of hands'. The image of the baby held securely in its mother's arms might translate to: welcoming individuals; giving a clear lead on task; modelling behaviour; engaging with what comes up in the group; conveying that feeling, including strong feeling, is OK and encouraging its translation into words.

Holding difficult feelings: using all the information about work

Many individuals, emotionally intelligent in their personal lives, believe that at work they must be completely 'logical' and remain emotionally unaffected by their experiences. To be 'businesslike' means to be unemotional. This mistaken idea leads people to cut themselves off from huge quantities of useful information about work, and so from crafting creative solutions to dilemmas.

Most of the emotion thus pushed away is uncomfortable in content. 'Holding' therefore includes 'containing difficult emotions' to allow group members to become aware of, digest and integrate them, and therefore able to use a broader range of information in their working lives. This 'containing' is a crucial part of holding. The coach conveys that difficult experiences can be borne, and their significance explored.[35] Here is an action learning set facilitator describing what she did when a group member began to cry in the first meeting of an action learning set. The learning experience was particularly powerful because the facilitator had herself had a similar experience as a set member:

> I just wanted to make her feel as comfortable as I could and to keep the group working and moving and I moved tissues towards her which I remember you doing with me actually and we waited and she was all very apologetic and saying everything that I'd said, I can't believe I'm crying, I didn't realize this was such an issue and we waited and

gave her a bit of space and time I suppose and when she was ready, she carried on.

Holding is an integrating process. It is the experiencing of emotion that allows it to shift, and so allows the person to 'move on'. The amplification of feeling in a group allows this process to surface readily. (See Chapter 3 for the processes through which this amplification takes place.) As they understand their feelings about work more fully, group members begin to discriminate feelings generated by work from those of a more personal origin. This allows individuals to decide how to act – or not to act – based on a fuller understanding, including emotional and social as well as intellectual and factual information.

Vignette: Holding a change process

The CEO of a small communications company needed to achieve cash savings and a more flexible approach in the face of very competitive market conditions. She hired a coach to help her manage the change. The coach encouraged her to explore her own frustrations and hopes about the business situation. This helped her overcome feelings of panic and helplessness. The next task was to break the news to two teams that their functions were to be merged, resulting in some redundancies and moves. The coach prepared the CEO to present the facts directly but compassionately, and 'take the flak'. He worked with her in a series of meetings with each team.

Initial feelings of anger, disbelief, worthlessness and powerlessness were expressed, followed by reluctant acceptance. Each individual re-examined their personal goals, and in the end the redundancies were all voluntary. At the end, the teams, CEO, directors and colleagues met to celebrate their contribution.

After a suitable break, the coach, who had become a trusted figure, began work with the new team to help them understand and organize themselves around their new, more fluid goals.

Feelings about work and personal life can easily become muddled. Today this is complex, not merely 'taking work home' or having less capacity at work because of domestic pressures. Arlie Hochschild writes about how personal time poverty, resulting from the high pressure of modern work, can create curious reversals in our allegiances to and feelings about work and home.[36]

In a group, members come to understand their work situations more fully, and to integrate what they feel and what they think about work challenges. As a result their ability to act is liberated, often quite dramatically compared with previous performance. This ability to act on a fuller analysis is the core of the greater confidence and effectiveness that group participants report. It is not therapy, since it is focused on the-person-in-work-role, and yet its effects are (small-t) therapeutic, in that members perform better and feel better about their performance.

Holding as time goes on

In the early days of a group, the group coach must shoulder much responsibility for the group's sense of safety. As a group matures, members develop confidence that the group is a safe place. Repeated experiences of safety with difficult subjects, and sharing struggles, in time make the group itself feel safe.

Holding is an unintrusive process. It requires the self-restraint to wait to see what the group can do without jumping in too quickly to offer help. It links with the development of interpersonal skills in the group members. Three people training as group coaches were asked later about the skills they had gained. Here are their answers:

> I count to two before I jump in with questions, because I know I can think too fast . . . it's important to slow down so other people have a chance.

> I control myself better from jumping in with both feet, not as well as I'd like to but better.

> Speaking less. Directing less. Becoming more comfortable with silence.

This restraint allows something very important to happen. Whereas at the start of the group the role of the group coach requires at least some active leadership to create a sense of safety, as time goes on, the group itself takes over this role; members become more active and competent in the group process. Repeated experiences of being held *by the group* enhance the security and sense of acceptance: 'acceptance is the keyword',[37] and the group itself can then become 'the container that helps transform incoherent and unconscious perceptions into coherent thought'.[38]

Vignette: The phrasing of an intervention

The action learning set was helping Helen plan for promotion. Her career had been 'on hold' since the tragic death of her partner a few years before. A senior post was coming up, but Helen had convinced herself that she would interview badly.

JENNY: That seems unlikely, you always appear so professional – what would stop you appearing professional in the interview?

HELEN: I'm afraid I will freeze, be unable to talk.

MEL: What could you do that would make you feel more confident?

HELEN: I'm not sure.

COACH: What has helped you in these situations before?

HELEN: Being very well prepared, thinking through all the questions, and remembering to slow down my breathing and moving beforehand and as I go in.

The group had accurately pinpointed Helen's dilemma, but their future-oriented questions were increasing her anxiety. A traumatic loss had made it difficult for her to focus on the future. By tilting the focus of the question to positive past experiences, the coach enabled Helen to reconnect with her capability.

The role of the group coach gradually becomes more unobtrusive, quietly attending to the group while the group attends to the work – available if needed, but generally less active, involving maintenance, help with overcoming new or reappearing obstacles, and refining and deepening communication. This requires a deeper understanding of the nine group processes to which we will turn in the next chapter.

What enables the group coach to hold a group effectively?

In this chapter we have covered several elements of the group coach's behaviour, and how it must change over time. What does not change, though intervention may be more rarely needed, is the group coach's role as the boundary-keeper, the person who holds the framework within which the group works. Although using psychological concepts, the group coach's role is very practical:

- focus on self-at-work
- personal links under the control of the person concerned
- communicating that all feelings are allowed
- tolerating the feelings oneself
- ability and willingness to voice the feelings
- encouraging the exploration of feelings
- asking about the distinction between feeling and action
- helping members link problems, new information and action.

Notice that the group coach, like the individual coach, focuses on the group's task mainly indirectly, by promoting group members' capacities to tackle it. This is a guideline, not a straitjacket. There are times when the group coach shares insights or information to move the task along. But this will be incidental, and usually explicitly book-marked as a brief stepping out of role. The primary focus is on helping the group to move the task forward by concentrating on the quality of interactions in the group. If the group coach is seduced into focusing on the group's task rather than her/his own, which is to help the group improve its functioning, then the group and its task will be the loser.

For the group coach to hold a group, s/he must feel confident that s/he can keep the group safe and productive for its members. Such confidence is based on the experience of having been held in groups, previous experiences of working productively with groups, and having one's work with the group held. Training, practice and supervision are key.

Exchange

'Exchange' is the encounter with what is new, different or previously unknown in one's experience. Difference carries information. Without difference there is no change and no development; yet without some sense of common ground there is nowhere safe to stand while you are challenged. You can only engage with difference in a sufficiently holding context.

Exchange in a group has many advantages over exchange in a one-to-one relationship.[39] There is a far wider range of opportunities for productive learning. It is 'on the level', that is, an equal exchange between members of a group, which many people find easier to swallow than coach/client feedback. The reality testing of several perspectives also greatly increases the probability of accurate feedback.

Vignette: Unanimous feedback

Graham regularly caused extra work for everyone because he never thought ahead. Various individuals, including Carol, the team manager, had taken this up with him, but with little effect. In a team coaching session one day he was talking about an event that had 'gone pear-shaped' and commented 'I suppose I could have got that part sorted in advance' about one of the crucial details. 'That's right!' was the emphatic response from everyone else in the circle. 'But I'm not that bad at forward planning' he protested. The coach said nothing. Nor did anyone else. There was a moment's pause, and then someone began to giggle. Graham looked round, and a smile crept across his face as everyone began to laugh. Helpless to protest, he laughed too. 'Bang to rights' he said. 'OK, what do you want me to do differently the next time?'

The acceptance that Graham simultaneously felt while receiving critical feedback made the experience tolerable. Notice that the coach did nothing active; s/he simply got out of the way and allowed the group to take care of the necessary feedback.

The 'aha' moments we occasionally experience are only one aspect of exchange: 'aha' moments are moments of reordering information in a new pattern.[40] The genuine lightbulb moment is a profound experience indicating a deep-seated reorganization of our perceptions, but is not the common currency of exchange. It isn't usually one 'Damascus Road' exchange that makes the difference. It is the continuous iterative process of taking in new information, a different 'explanation', with its implications. The process is constant, and as a result can become invisible.

> It was more the experience of being part of a group and sticking with it when I could have left quite easily . . . more the whole process of being part of the group rather than the particular moment in time.

New thinking in psychological fields understands individual identity as a process, shifting through time, not a fixed quantity.[41] Exchange is the process that allows identity to be formed and reformed through innumerable small identifications and distinctions. The repetition of the group process gradually allows more acceptance of our individual foibles, so that idiosyncrasies are acknowledged and accepted, sometimes non-verbally:

> people would look at each other and everyone would have a bit of a giggle, but actually it's quite helpful because that's the sort of stuff you reflect on at a later date.

> it's a certain amount of acceptance and being given, yeah people giving you a bit of a nudge and an elbow about it, but saying actually it's quite funny but you are a bit peculiar and yes, that's good.

Although words are an aspect of exchange, meaning can be seen here to be communicated non-verbally, relying on the pre-verbal learning processes and emotional attunement which so enrich the life of groups. Words for the exchange will arise spontaneously in the group, but the recipient of the feedback has already been prepared by the non-verbal communications. It relies on the 'implicit knowing' discussed earlier.

Conventionalized exchange in action learning sets and team coaching

This gradual exchange develops over time. Where time is more limited, other conventions are adopted to encourage a more direct encounter with difference. For example, in action learning, the core activities are listening and questioning. Questioning is the primary medium of exchange. It is impossible for the questioners to determine in advance which of their questions will be experienced by the presenter as challenging; the challenge is where the presenter finds it. The task for the questioners is to respond increasingly sensitively to the presenter's cues, dropping or pursuing a line of questioning according to its value to the presenter.

In action learning questioning is balanced by listening, which seems to provide the holding that allows the method to work so well. Practised rigorously, action learning is robust. Even relatively inexperienced group coaches can hold challenging material in the group if they stick to its conventions. Action learning is discussed in Chapter 7.

There seem to be two further factors that make the challenge of being questioned bearable. There is the fact that it is shared, so that everyone undergoes the same experience – sometimes supportive, sometimes an ordeal, sometimes both. And there is the fact that it is time-limited.

These factors are also critical in using feedback tools with teams.[42]

When working with teams, there are literally hundreds of possible tools, offering a framework for understanding (see 'Using teams tools and models in coaching' in Chapter 6). These tools seem to have at least three purposes: to offer a conceptual model that more or less usefully (over)simplifies reality, to depersonalize and reduce threat in what may be quite sensitive feedback, and to 'kick-start' a conversation about how individual differences hamper and help communication and therefore the team's performance.

The tools alone will not do the trick. The group coach's capacity to 'hold' difficult conversations is indispensable in using tools to promote feedback with teams. The usefulness of a structured approach also requires calm, reassuring leadership, even-handedness and clear time boundaries.

Final remarks about exchange

In human relationships, exchange is of value in itself independent of any content, because from the earliest days of life, before words, it communicates the relationship: you cannot talk *about* anything to a baby, but the exchange is known to be of value.[43] When mothers and babies communicate, there is patterning of variations on a theme; the sense of belonging and acceptance is reinforced simultaneously with the experience of difference, through the rhythms of play.

There are many kinds of exchange, and 'calling a spade a shovel' or 'saying what has not been said' are only one kind of challenge. Many challenges in the intimate medium of a group are unspoken, known only to the person who has noticed and taken in, at first non-consciously, some aspect of another person's reality.

It is in the group, paradoxically, that we can be most fully ourselves. We become aware that other people feel differently to us, laugh at different things – but that no one way is better than another.[44] It is our differences that define our individuality. The experience of 'groupness' allows individuals to feel secure enough to risk self-revelation, and therefore the possibility of encountering some feedback that might influence them and allow a choice to change.[45]

> Getting feedback about how I present myself to the world, and hearing how others assumed me to be one sort of person, who was now emerging as quite different, was interesting and surprising.

In this chapter we have reviewed the processes involved in human learning and how well-held groups can amplify the process of feedback and exchange. In the next chapter we examine the group processes through which this occurs.

Looking deeper: the secret life of groups

Part 2's opening page (p. 21) shows how this chapter links to group themes overall.

Nine group processes
Group matrix
Communication
Translation
Mirroring
Exchange
Resonance
Condenser phenomena
Location
The reflection process

This chapter

In the previous chapter we looked at two essential processes in learning, holding and exchange. In this chapter we examine nine fundamental processes in group life. Understanding these enables practitioners to design better interventions, both with teams and with learning groups. As you read, compare the ideas and examples to your own experiences in groups, to help make sense of what is presented.

This chapter contains:
- This chapter
- Nine group processes
- The coach's task and the group's task
- Group matrix
- Communication
- Translation
- Mirroring
- Negative mirroring
- Exchange
- Resonance
- Condenser phenomena
- Location
- The reflection process

Nine group processes

The chapter examines nine elemental processes of group dynamics (see above), processes we experience in groups, that contribute to our total experience of the group.

The processes are in themselves neither positive nor negative – they just are. The task of the group coach is to understand and work with them to hold the group in a productive balance between safety and challenge. The balance is different in every group, and the coach needs skill to attune to a particular group's capacity. The more mature a group is, the more it is able to tolerate its own differences, discords and negative aspects, secure in the knowledge that it is basically a 'good team'. Therefore what might be a destructive experience in a new group can be a profound learning experience in a more mature group.

The nine processes are active in *all* groups, including teams. Examples are given in the text, but test what is said from your own knowledge: weigh up the concepts in the light of your group experiences.

The concepts derive mainly from the study of groups undertaken by group analysts over the past seventy years.

Group analysis was first developed, by S.H. Foulkes and his colleagues, as a therapy of individuals via group interaction, and today is applied in psychotherapy, training, professional development and organizational consultation. Group analytic theory blends psychoanalytic insights with Gestalt, systemic and other social-scientific perspectives, and focuses on the integration of the individual in her/his network of relationships, resulting in better personal functioning and interpersonal relating.

In writing this chapter I thought about whether to change the 'technical' terms to something more 'user-friendly', but decided that in most cases there probably was no term more user-friendly than the original. Some of the concepts, such as 'mirroring' and 'resonance', are so apt that they have entered the language and begun to be used in common parlance. There is a risk here, because some of the terms have a precise technical meaning but a more generalized conversational one, which may be misunderstood by the reader-who-skims. One good example is 'communication'.

The coach's task and the group's task

The coach and the group have different tasks. The group is working to achieve its goals. The coach is working to enable the *group* to achieve its goals: the group itself is the coach's field. The first step is a fuller understanding of what can be observed in the interactions. The practitioner can then use her/his perceptions to design interventions suitable to the receptiveness and level of awareness of that group. S/he needs self-restraint, and a light hand.

Generally you would not identify these nine group processes with clients, although sharing the insights they provide is powerful. The concepts themselves, psychological processes happening between people in groups, are mainly helpful for the group practitioner to have in mind, in gaining a fuller understanding of 'what is really happening' in the group.

Team/group members are rightly focused on *their* task, and may be far from interested in the study of groups. Of course, in many instances the group could benefit from greater understanding of *how* they work, but it has to be at a level meaningful to them. This accounts for the popularity and value of conceptual tools such as Myers-Briggs Type Indicator and Belbin (see Chapter 6, 'Using team tools and models in coaching', which offers a simple 'road map' to some widely used tools). The drawback is that any conceptual tool lends itself to a rather static and limited view of what is going on. Reality is likely to be a good deal more dynamic and complex.

In a short-term piece of work, or with a team very resistant to the discussion of its dynamics, the interventions of the group practitioner should focus on removing obstacles to that task (such as helping individuals who rub each other up the wrong way to negotiate a way of cooperating), or contribute to the task (such as reinforcing positive, task-achieving behaviour). See 'Process breaks and process skills' in Chapter 9. You are 'fixing' the communication while you are present, and the problems are likely to re-emerge after you leave. If you are working with a team over the medium or longer term, it becomes possible to increase the team's awareness of how their relationship patterns help or hamper their work, so that they become more able to challenge themselves.

Group matrix

The concept 'group matrix' is more properly a collection of processes, the totality of a group's dynamics.[46]

In common parlance, people use the phrase 'group dynamics' as a kind of catch-all phrase when talking about several things at once, or a sense of 'what's happening underneath' in a group. Often the phrase is used when someone wants to convey that they *don't* understand what is going on, but have a sense that there is more going on than meets the eye. Because its use has become rather imprecise, the term itself has become less useful.

More useful is 'group matrix', both broader and more specific than 'group dynamics' in its meaning. The group matrix is made up of two elements, the *dynamic matrix* and the *foundation matrix*.

The *dynamic matrix* is the totality of communication

and experience in a particular group, over time; the sense of the group having a life, including memory and history, more than the sum of its individual parts. It cannot be fully understood without including the element of time, through which things are inevitably dynamic, subject to change. The dynamic matrix includes everything that is said, felt and experienced by any member and between members in the group over time, and the relationship effects of these patterns of communication. It includes what is conscious, what is unconscious and what is 'non-conscious' but implicitly known and communicated. It is 'dynamic' because it is constantly developing and deepening as further communications, connections and shifts in relationship patterning take place.

The *foundation matrix* is a broader concept referring to our common biological and cultural heritage as humans, the parts of our experience that can be 'taken as read'. It includes Jung's idea of the collective unconscious (a primordial reservoir of symbols of psychological and relational patterns), and also non-conscious but normally shared cultural assumptions, such as 'children and older people should be taken care of'. How deep-seated an assumption is is revealed when someone transgresses it: we are deeply shocked by the ill-treatment of children.

The extent and the limitations of the foundation matrix are most visible in cross-cultural groups. Although as members of the same species we share some common assumptions, the interpretation of the axiom 'children and older people should be taken care of' varies from culture to culture, with wide differences in the degree of respect accorded to the elderly, or the expectations placed on children.

The concept of the group matrix fundamentally changes our understanding of consciousness in a group. The 'interacting processes' between the people in the group create a new, shared and co-created group consciousness.

This view of things is both revolutionary and at the same time very practical for the group coach. It means that each person in the room is both an individual and a part of a larger entity. What they communicate has a personal meaning, but potentially also expresses a meaning shared by the group as a whole.

With this in mind, we have a new window on every communication. What does it mean for the individual? What
might it mean for the group as a whole? We can look for
repeated similar communications, perhaps made in a variety of ways. We can ask the group about the connections
between shared or similar meanings, which will have the
effect of building the group's cohesiveness. We can refrain
from labelling individuals as troublesome or resistant until
we have understood the *group* meaning on which their individual behaviour is a variation. A common example might be
where one person verbally expresses boredom or frustration,
but only after others have expressed the same in different
ways – looking disengaged, checking their text messages,
tapping their feet.

At the same time, to be aware of individuals as individuals is crucial: the group coach must consider individual
and group development together. Groups are powerful
sources of individual learning, because the resources of
the whole group are available to the individual members.
Paradoxically, it is in a well-functioning group that we can
be most fully ourselves, understanding ourselves by contrast
and comparison with others. As we gradually come to realize, with head, heart and gut, that 'different from' does not
automatically mean 'better than' or 'worse than', we become
more able to be ourselves. It is the close contact with others
that creates self-awareness.

The group matrix, and all the other concepts in this
chapter except the 'reflection process',[47] are derived from
Foulkes' writings. The next, and perhaps most elemental, is
communication.

Communication

'Communication' is a word commonly used in a variety of
ways, many of them inexact. It is used here in a precise sense,
as 'unit of meaning' – an event in the life of the group, however small, that may have a meaning.

Everything that happens in a group, not just what is
said, can be regarded as a potential communication.[48] This
means that the group coach must entertain the possibility

that everything is significant. Many of the skills s/he uses to apprehend communications are those of bringing into her/his own conscious awareness the 'implicit knowing' described at the beginning of Chapter 2.

Communications can include:

- facial expression
- facial movements
- looks
- eye contact
- who looks at whom and how frequently
- emotional tone
- unarticulated emotional content
- sounds
- pace of speech
- inflection of speech
- tone of speech
- volume of speech
- intensity of speech
- frequency of speech
- muttering, whispering and asides
- who speaks to whom and how frequently
- who is and who is not included as a member
- gestures
- bodily movement
- style of movement
- angle of body
- body position – habitual and unusual
- choice of clothes
- tee-shirt slogans/images
- other aspects of appearance
- degree of energy in movement or in expressions or other signals
- degree of animation
- late arrival
- early arrival
- messages – content, where sent, timing
- interruptions – internal to group, such as mobile phones
- interruptions – external, such as non-members coming in
- bringing/not bringing notes/equipment
- early departure
- late departure.

Communications are not always straightforward to interpret. Leaning forward, for instance, could indicate a high degree of engagement, a frustration so intense that what the person really wants to do is stand up and leave, or it could mean that the person cannot hear what is said. Speech is influenced by regional accents or intonation, and by whether or not the language spoken is a mother tongue. There can be no wall chart that infallibly interprets every gesture and nuance. Context is paramount in construing meaning.

The skill of the group coach is to notice patterns (much of this 'noticing' might not be conscious), repeated or shared communications that might hold meaning for the group. Knowledge of the group's context is also important here – is there anything in the context that sheds light on this communication? Communications made in a variety of modalities – with the eyes, with the inflection of speech, with physical movement or its intensity – that seem to confirm each other are worth taking up with the group in the form that makes them shared – by putting the question into words, or 'translating' it. The group coach needs insight, sometimes courage, and openness to the possibility that s/he might be wrong. Or right.

Should all communications be made verbal? Well, they couldn't possibly be. In any group there are innumerable small communications going on in any five-minute period. Most of the time, most of us don't notice most of what is going on. This is always true in a group – no one can notice everything, and it is not possible to take up every communication.

Accepting this can be liberating – since no one can notice more than a fraction of 'what is really going on', the important thing is to notice persistent, prevalent and repeated behaviours that may be important communications. Our inbuilt sensors for 'implicit knowing' help us here, and these can be greatly enhanced through experiential training and supervision.

Translation

Translation is the intricate process of 'putting into words' communications made in some other way, making the communications ever more articulate.

For better or worse, we are verbal creatures, subject to the 'double-edged sword of language',[49] which both allows us to share our experience and forever reduces our experience to what can be communicated in words. Translation is the process of slowly making conscious meaning from both unconscious[50] and non-conscious communications. It is done by piecing together communications made over time and perhaps by different members.[51]

The process is one of rendering communication more and more articulate as time goes on. Early on the group coach gives a lead in this area, and her/his skills remain available to the group; over time, however, the group will make increasing sense of its own communications, accessing a far wider range of information than was available at first. The distancing effect of the 'double-edged sword of language' offers the advantage of greater objectivity:

> putting things into words meant I could stand outside and look in.

Mirroring

Mirroring[52] is everywhere in groups. It does not mean conscious imitation or matching, but refers to non-conscious or unconscious processes. In any situation, we non-consciously compare current encounters and occurrences with previous experiences, in order to make sense of them. Put simply, we are looking for 'like' and 'not like' (mirroring) and also 'other than' (exchange). Because these processes are everywhere, they can be very easy to overlook. Mirroring includes processes of projection and of transference, which are explained near the start of Chapter 2, but mirroring is also central to all relating.

The recent discovery of mirror neurons suggests a physical–scientific base for 'mirroring', a concept established in the psychological sciences for many years. These neurons fire when we do something, *and* when we watch the same action performed by another, if we have already learned how to do it. This is powerfully demonstrated as we observe sports fans.

Mirror neurons provide the mechanism through which we 'connect by watching' and feel empathy, and may be the brain's way of deciphering visual stimuli so that we can relate to the world. Some scientists believe that mirror neurons connect to the limbic (or emotional) system, and are the physical mechanism through which we tune into each other's feelings: a fundamental part of our brain's architecture, dedicated to connecting with the minds of others.[53]

Mirroring occurs in at least four different ways.

1 *Being seen, accepted, recognized and acknowledged as oneself.* This first aspect of mirroring is closely related to holding, and thus crucial in achieving that sense of safety that allows us to engage fully with challenges and differences. Some people have more, some less, capacity to receive this kind of mirroring. It originates in our earliest relationship as babies, where we need to be seen and valued – 'I am reflected, therefore I exist'. In groups, mirroring in an atmosphere of sympathy and identification enhances feelings of self-worth.[54]

Mothers' mirroring interactions with their babies are not exact, but play with variation – of expression, pace, intensity. It is this variation that groups are so good at replicating, because the mirroring is varied through several pairs of eyes, and is shared and mutual. Most of this mirroring happens non-verbally, and it happens all the time. This is the primary mechanism through which the group comes to 'hold' the individual in a well-functioning group.

2 *The experience of 'that's like me' or 'I feel that too'.* As we listen to someone else's story, we *identify* with another person or people. The identification is rarely total; individual variations on the theme will be felt, and sometimes expressed. This aspect of mirroring, like the next, is closely aligned with the process of projection (see Chapter 2).

3 *Seeing aspects of ourselves in interaction with others in the group*. Sometimes these are aspects of ourselves we are less keen on:

> I was really surprised when Christine said that I was doing the 'Yes but . . .' thing that I was berating Mike for.

Over time this allows each individual to gain a more realistic self-image; the same member commented:

> I'm beginning to think that being part of an Action Learning Set is like being in a hall of funny mirrors. You can see things about other people quite clearly and every now and then you get something resembling a reflection, sometimes distorted in shape or size. By seeing the way other people deal with things and recognizing certain traits, you can also recognize things (identical, similar or contrasting), perhaps for the first time, in yourself.

4 Strong mutual feelings between two or more members of the group, based on some degree of identification or disidentification (for example a strong sympathy, admiration, irritation or dislike).

These feelings are often *transferential* (see Chapter 2). Mirroring is both positive and negative; normal (i.e. not excessive) positive mirroring is the 'glue' in any group, but negative mirroring will be the source of many of the obstacles we encounter, particularly in working with teams.

Negative mirroring

Negative mirroring is most likely to arise in the third and fourth of our types of mirroring, where projection or transference are involved. In (3) above, someone sees in another member of the group some aspect of themselves that they dislike and are generally more or less able to avoid recognizing. In a group where feedback is honest, the multiple reality checks make it difficult to keep the illusion, so the person experiences pressure to re-own their disowned (projected – see Chapter 2) characteristic and adjust their self-image.

In (4) above, someone experiences the same relationship patterns with another group member that they have experienced with someone important (perhaps a parent or sibling) from early in life.

This is not the same as 'you are just like my friend Jane'. It is about the way the group member experienced that original relationship, and the persistence of that relationship pattern. It is transference (see also Chapter 2). Other people's transference is much easier to spot than our own: at times we have all found ourselves in a relationship where we are called upon to play a part for which we have not auditioned. Consider a normally constructive manager who finds himself being uncharacteristically critical towards a team member who regards him as overbearing, 'just like my father'. It is harder to spot how we do the same to others.

Negative mirror reactions can be destructive in a learning group, and even more so in a team working closely. The task of the group coach is to bring reality to bear, to help the individuals re-own the mirrored characteristic; or, failing that, at least to negotiate a way of collaborating in the face of ongoing mutual misunderstanding. In a long-standing team, there may be a number of these processes occurring at once.

In a business context, negative mirror reactions can pose a considerable challenge for the team coach, who is not, after all, there as a therapist. It is all too easy either to overstep the boundaries of the relationship *or* to give the problem insufficient attention. Further, if interventions do achieve improvement, the individuals concerned have plenty of opportunity for mutual backsliding when the coach is not there. If the unconscious pay-offs from continuing with the destructive behaviour outweigh the factors supporting change, over time they will undermine any improvements.

The multiple perspectives of the group can be helpful in achieving improved understanding of the present, and so helping individuals to disentangle present reality from their personal past. Sometimes this will be enough to resolve things, but not always. If the negative mirroring experience is particularly powerful, the team members caught in it may need additional support to manage themselves in relation to each other, in order to contribute fully to the work of the team. A first step is to get everyone's agreement that this would be a desirable goal.

Negative mirroring is particularly powerful when certain conditions are fulfilled.

Factors amplifying negative mirroring reactions

- The mirroring is unconscious (we are unaware of the link between your characteristics and mine, or my history and the present)
- It is mutual (for instance, you believe that I am arrogant and overbearing, and I believe that you are)
- The characteristic I am being challenged to face in myself is one of which I am ashamed
- Different types of mirroring are present (e.g. the link between your characteristics, mine, and the past experience of us both has not been made)
- Type 3 and type 4 mirroring are both present, redoubling the effect.

Exchange

The concept of *exchange* as an overarching fundamental process is explored in 'Exchange' in Chapter 2. 'Exchanges' are units of exchange, the innumerable small interactions through which group members take in new information. Exchange is everywhere, invisible precisely because we are surrounded by it.

Whereas mirroring is understood as primarily an experience of similarity (including negative mirroring, which is a denial of similarity), exchanges are an encounter with what is other, different or new[55] to us. In other words, mirroring is the experience of 'like' and 'not like', whereas exchange is the experience of 'other than'.

In a group, feedback arises spontaneously between members, and is more acceptable because of the relative equality in power; group members can give each other direct feedback that a coach would have to think carefully about conveying.

Vignette: Shut up already

In the social services team, Colin had a remarkable ability to turn the conversation so he 'had the floor'. His
colleagues thought they had tried everything. As Harry
described a particularly harrowing case in a team supervision session, Colin interrupted again with a case of
his own. Arthur snapped. 'You're doing it again! You
thought Harry had had enough time, and you were
determined to get in.' Colin demurred, saying that he
wanted to help Harry. Every other member of the team
gave Colin the same feedback, mostly rather more gently
than Arthur. The supervisor said nothing, since the team
were doing fine without his help. Colin was rather silent
for a while, and over the next few months seemed to
regulate himself better and use a fairer share of the
team's supervision time.

Resonance

Resonance is the felt sense of links between members' experiences including their emotional content, resulting in a
deeper mutual understanding. The image is of musical resonance at different pitches, where the after-tones reverber-
ate. When someone else says something that seems to have
real meaning for me, apart from the meaning for them, that is
'resonance'. My response reflects my habitual personal style
of responding,[56] and each person's response is a variation on
the theme.

> Highlights are when you recognize things that are just
> repeated themes that you feel and identify with and you
> realize that other people can identify with as well.

It is an intuitive, largely unconscious process, not an intellectual one, and arises from the predispositions and psychological make-up of the specific group members. Because the
'echoes' are sounded by the individuals in that group, its

precise expression will be different in every group. For group members to translate their sense of what is resonant into words strengthens group cohesiveness and the sense of being held.

Resonance works as members tell each other stories that touch each other and lead to a 'chain' of related stories. Through the telling the individuals understand each other better – the team or learning group is 'built'.

This process arises naturally and cannot be forced, because it does not arise through conscious choice. When it does arise, it creates bonds between group members, but it cannot be manipulated. The group coach should tread carefully: openness cannot be switched from zero to maximum in one go. Team exercises designed to increase openness, therefore, should be chosen or crafted to offer choice about the level at which participants engage: an opportunity, not a demand. The choice of how much to reveal must explicitly reside with the individuals. Small-scale risk-taking in some members 'encourages the others' and gradually produces stronger links and greater risks.

Condenser phenomena

Condenser phenomena[57] refer to shifts in the group, a release of tension as previously unconscious or hidden material is shared, often through metaphor and symbolic ideas in the discussion. As group members pool their associations, new meanings emerge, the symbol acting as a condenser (or intensifier).

Vignette: Everyday condenser phenomenon

In the pub Bill began talking about how he had been 'done over' by HQ; others chipped in with their experiences, and the atmosphere grew more and more indignant. Everyone had a hard luck story to tell, and no one had got any satisfaction, but there was a twisted satisfaction in talking about it. Everyone went back to work

> satisfied – they worked for a 'rubbish' organization and were powerless to do anything about it, but at least they were all in it together.

The metaphor of 'victim' was the one around which this phenomenon organized itself, with unfortunate results for the organization.

There is an element of surprise in the condenser phenomenon, a 'charge' released which feels greater than could be predicted rationally. Such phenomena can arise through the sharing of non-rational material, or through the deepening of resonance in a mature group. Self-revelation is often the trigger, particularly of something that feels quite risky. Everyone is relieved by the possibility of speaking about what was previously kept quiet, and further disclosures by other members are likely, moving the group's interaction to a deeper level.

Vignette: Shift to another level

Barbara shared some ethical concerns about her coaching practice in the supervision group. She was surprised and reassured by the depth of the group's response and engagement with the issues she presented, and in the ensuing discussion other members shared similar concerns in an atmosphere of increased freedom.

Evidence of condenser phenomena is experienced in the intensity of engagement, a sense of release and in a 'chain' of associations being assembled, each member contributing a link.

Location

Location is the principle that every event, even if it appears to be confined to one or two people in a group, involves the group as a whole in some way.[58] This principle is derived from the Gestalt idea of figure (foreground) and ground (background). In practice it refers to the capacity of a group to 'locate' a particular characteristic with one individual, so that that person seems to be the only or main person in the group expressing it; examples are aggression, expertise or victimhood.

Over time people can acquire a particular 'role' in a group – 'Mr Angry', 'the expert' or 'eternal victim' – which, if they become fixed, are problematic. The problem is both the individual's, in being too identified with the characteristic, and the rest of the group's, in being cut off from that characteristic which is 'carried' by one individual.

The 'located' characteristics are by no means always negative in themselves: for instance, one person may be or become 'The Oracle', the fount of all knowledge. This too can have a negative effect if the role gets too 'stuck' – no one else feels much responsibility to have or acquire information, and they are rescued from the discomforts of 'not knowing'; The Oracle, on the other hand, may be tempted to pretend to more knowledge than they actually possess.

Where the disowned idea or characteristic is deeply unconscious among the other members, the difficulty is more acute. Perhaps only one person voices an unpalatable feeling that others share only unconsciously. The member who expresses it is a 'sensitive', a canary in the coal mine, and risks being stuck with it if the group fails in its task of re-owning what has been repudiated. The unwanted feeling or pattern then appears to belong only to the member expressing it.

Vignette: Location and scapegoating

Fred was the only member of the regional managers' group who was willing to acknowledge how incompetent and overwhelmed he sometimes felt in the face of the quarterly demand for detailed strategic plans backed by data. Fred was experienced, but unassuming. The group was composed of mostly newer managers who did not feel secure enough to admit feeling daunted, even to themselves. An idea developed that Fred's team was underperforming. Over time this idea filtered upwards and Fred was challenged on performance more than anyone else at his level.

A coach was hired to work with Fred on his performance. As part of this exercise they compared Fred's preparation of reports, and actual results, with those of other regional teams. They discovered that Fred's region was broadly on a par with the others in complying with the directors' demands, and actually better than average measured on performance.

Location is the first step towards possible scapegoating, and the fear of it is important in keeping people from straightforward communication, as in the example. If people are unable to re-own the parts of themselves that at times feel overwhelmed or incompetent, the member who can do so can get stuck with it, and become a scapegoat for the weaknesses of all.

Fred was a canary, ahead of the crowd. His ability to face his feelings was a sign of his professional maturity, also demonstrated in better actual results. He was different from the others in being more experienced, and envy may have been a factor in his being targeted.

The coach went on to work with the managers' group to help them collaborate more effectively. As the group matured and more people were able to acknowledge feelings and pool expertise, the reporting compliance increased from 64% to 82% and actual performance improved by a few percentage points in all regions.

At times there will be individuals in a team who are seriously out of step with everyone else, but the group coach should always cast a sceptical eye on any formulation that makes a particular individual 'the problem'. How convenient for everyone else that there is someone who is 'worse' than they are! And that they can do nothing to improve things, since it is someone else's fault! See also 'Limiting scapegoating and other destructive behaviour' in Chapter 4.

We have already noted that we humans have a deep-rooted fear of 'bad' group experiences. Because of the power of the group to amplify all experience, through the processes outlined in this chapter, destructive experiences have greater power in the group. It is a key part of the group coach's role to have a weather eye to each individual to minimize harm (see the section mentioned above). There is a fine art here. Difficult experiences may be developmental for individuals or the group because they test the safety of the group, and give an opportunity to understand and own 'bad' feelings. This can generate relief as we realize we are not alone in having these feelings, and energy is no longer tied up with repressing our own anger, contempt or hostility. This shift may in itself create an opportunity for reaching a more con-structive state. But it is only in a securely held and relatively mature group that this kind of transition is possible, and individuals have differing capacities for tolerating their own 'badness'. If in doubt, it is generally best for the group coach to err on the side of minimizing harm, provided s/he attends carefully to what happens next. Even if s/he is over-protective, the group will soon give a 'steer' if they are ready to take greater risks.

The reflection process

This last process is very useful in learning and supervision groups, and is discussed more fully in Chapter 8. The reflection process arises as someone tells a story or recounts a conversation, and the group picks up on and feels its dynamic, including emotional content of which the storyteller was previously not conscious. The feelings of the players in the story are felt by the members of the group; if expressed, these make new information available to the storyteller.

In the group context, the emotional content is amplified, and so becomes more available. The group picks up on more facets of the story, and the reflection of dominant emotions by several people makes the experience more powerful than in individual coaching. There are obvious links with mirror-ing, in the recreation of experience from elsewhere in the here and now of the group.

Here are two group members' comments on the reflection process in action.

Vignette: Reflection after the learning group 1

During the discussion I realized just how frustrated I've become at my time being wasted by the lack of planning and coherence. I also later started to think that my policy of 'going my own sweet way' and simply doing the things I wanted was possibly not such a complete solution as I'd supposed. I also realized that incidents such as the one I brought to the first meeting – i.e. being expected to sort out problems that I would not have created – have, over the years, undermined my natural optimism and *joie de vivre*. I've taken to moaning about work for the first time in my life. I ran this past my husband later who agreed, and said it was driving him crazy (me too, now I admit it).

Vignette: Reflection after the learning group 2

I was surprised by others' reactions in my turn. I had felt that my problem was a technical issue, i.e. what behaviour to use, but others' reactions made me realize that it is a much deeper issue. I felt as if others were expressing the frustration that I am not allowing myself to express. This was helpful as I didn't realize how much I depended on the group to provide feedback and a yard-stick which allowed me to 'feel'.

This 'reflection process' is a fundamental tool in supervision,[59] and is also called 'parallel process'. It is a powerful tool for learning provided it is used carefully. See also Chapter 8.

In this chapter we have reviewed nine elemental group processes. In the next chapter we go on to examine eight factors that contribute in groups to learning and change.

Eight group factors influencing learning and change

Part 2's opening page (p. 21) shows how this
chapter links to group themes overall.

Eight group factors
Connectedness and belonging
Interpersonal learning
Competition, envy and admiration
Idealization and emulation
Practising courage
Witnessing and being witnessed
Encouragement
Group performance coaching

This chapter

Chapter 4 builds on Chapter 3 by adding eight group factors that contribute to learning to the nine group processes discussed there. The eight group factors are all routes to learning and change. The chapter, and Part 2, closes with a discussion of the group coach's role.

As with Chapter 3, the ideas are primarily concerned with the relationships between people, present in all groups, and in our two working categories, 'learning groups' and 'teams' alike. The group coach who recognizes these processes can work with them to foster success.

The eight group factors

The eight factors for change described here are commonly encountered features of group life. To focus on them can be of practical help

This chapter contains:
- This chapter
- The eight group factors
- Connectedness and belonging
- Interpersonal learning
- Competition, envy and admiration
- Idealization and emulation
- Practising courage
- Witnessing and being witnessed
- Encouragement
- Group performance coaching
- The roles of the group coach
  - Boundary keeper
  - Student of the group's interactions
  - Representing authority/experience in the group
  - Limiting scapegoating and other destructive behaviour
  - System administrator
- What are the characteristics of an effective group coach?
- Finally: Concluding Part 2

to the group coach wrestling with the complexities of her/his work. The factors are derived from my research into group factors that contribute to confidence and competence in group members.[60]

These factors depend on the group processes already described; that is, they happen through those processes. The boundaries between them are not rigid – they merge into each other somewhat, and are found together, not separated as they must be in a book. Nor are all the factors the same kind of thing. Some are things the group members gain (such as courage); some are the processes through which they gain them, either individually (witnessing) or as a group (group performance coaching). The concept of connectedness encapsulates the fact that the many acts of giving and receiving in any group are in themselves beneficial to the individual.

The group coach can nurture the positive use of these factors – but must do so by example, unobtrusively and with a light hand. The skills of a group coach are far removed from those of the cheerleader; much of the skill resides in knowing when to act and when to get out of the way.

Connectedness and belonging

A sense of belonging: 'everyone can recognize it but apparently no one can describe it'.[61] The innate sense of connectedness that we share is linked to group processes already described and about to be described.

In a recent qualitative study of action learning,[62] the sense of belonging and mutual support was rated by most members as the most important factor in a successful learning experience, whether or not members' actual experience had been successful. This finding is consistent with a body of research on group therapy that emphasizes the importance of cohesion.[63]

Connectedness, or the sense of belonging, is linked closely with 'holding' (Chapter 2): a well-held group feels 'connected' and has an overall sense of forward movement, of members making progress. This is true both in learning groups and in teams.

The sense of belonging to something worthwhile sets up a 'virtuous cycle', giving strength to members who use it to achieve greater individual maturity and autonomy. Members see their group as 'good' and identify with it, which boosts their confidence and their competence, as well as the opportunity to hone their capacities and skills through the work of the group.

Membership of a 'good' group is therefore experienced

as good in itself, additional to the gains through the work of the group. This seems to be primal, related to our origins as creatures who survived, individually and as a species, only by relating to each other in groups. Ethnographic, sociological and psychological studies, including studies of loneliness and severe recidivism, concur: belonging[64] is a human need. Being part of something larger which is good is reinternalized as a positive sense of self; members internalize the group atmosphere of acceptance, which augments an internal process of self-acceptance.

Vignette: Action learning for culture change through key individuals

A group was convened to train its members to facilitate action learning sets as part of a culture change programme throughout the organization. The self-selected members were all intelligent women, somewhat overqualified for their main roles. The process began with members joining together to experience action learning in their own set.

Members were very nervous at the outset of an eighteen-month process, but quickly found common ground and a depth of mutual knowledge through exploring work challenges. The speed of engagement was in part due to the homogeneity of the group. As members wrestled with frustrations arising from inadequate resources, mismanagement or lack of vision in their various departments, they discovered new ways of managing themselves, exercising leadership and building alliances in unexpected places. They became more adept at challenging poor practice and catalysing change.

The group itself, always seen as 'very good', became a powerhouse enabling all this. The group coach was idealized, but gradually members could differentiate more realistically what was her contribution and what was their own. The coach's willingness to be seen as fallible was important to this. The group achieved a mature and efficient working culture including a more balanced view of the contribution of the group coach, vital as they prepared in turn to facilitate their own sets. A year after the completion of the programme, all had moved to new roles that more fully used their capabilities to effect the desired culture change.

At the beginning, group members' confidence that 'this is a good group' is always to some degree an act of faith. The importance of the group coach setting the right tone cannot be overstated. S/he must be calm and confident *in the group*, and must model the kind of behaviour that is to become normal in the group as time goes on. As the group members have repeated experiences of the group providing something good, their act of faith is rewarded by the sense of belonging to something larger which is good, leading to greater individual confidence and courage in their work.

It is mirroring, identification and resonance that operate to strengthen these ties, and members can quickly form strong bonds with each other. Here is one person's account of how it feels:

real anger, really wanting to jump in there and say this is just not acceptable, what you've had to put up with or absolute wanting to just stand up and cheer at times and thinking I can't believe you did that, that's fantastic, an absolute delight for people that they've taken certain moves that have really worked out for them. . . . What does surprise me is that the rate, it seems to me that after spending not many hours with these people in a group, you can have very strong feelings of loyalty and comradeship.

When a new group is experienced as 'good' there is usually an element of idealization involved at first. Provided it is not extreme, this is functional, as it allows the group to get established, and helps members to maintain their commitment even when things get challenging; one member likened his group to physical exercise – 'it can be hard to make yourself do it but you know that it is good'. As the group matures the idealization is replaced by a more balanced view.

If a group gets stuck in idealization to maintain its cohesion, it cannot remain effective. It will distort reality to keep what is 'bad' firmly outside, an enemy that the group can unite to fight; or by scapegoating one or two members as embodying the 'bad' qualities that are not part of the group as a whole.

Many teams *permanently* maintain their cohesion at the expense of denigrating the wider organization of which they are part. This leads to poor communication and non-cooperation with other teams or departments, and is unlikely to produce good results for the wider enterprise.

If however the idealization is temporary, it can serve another kind of purpose. Systems theory teaches us that new ventures need to be protected from the system as a whole while they achieve viability. In the vignette above, the group saw itself as 'good' as against the organization as a whole, a stance fuelled by its homogeneity. The organization was then seen as 'bad' despite its support for the group. The group was learning a new way of working, the function of which in the wider organization was to challenge existing cultural assumptions. In the early stages this required a high level of cohesion for members to make the adjustment.

This allowed the members to grow stronger in a new way of working in a 'safe place' compartmentalized from the rest of the organization, before, paradoxically, going on to seed the new approach in the organization as a whole. It was a *temporary* stance that allowed group members to develop their new skills to viability, before launch of the wider programme.

Sometimes there are structural reasons why things are more likely to 'go wrong' at the point when a particular team is involved, for instance when production is delayed because of an accumulation of supply issues. This may result in feelings in that team not that it is 'good', but that it is 'bad', so that being part of that team undermines individuals' sense of self-worth; members are likely to have low commitment to the team and/or their task. If this gets stuck, such a team may unconsciously accept the role of being the 'bad' team that maintains things as they are by allowing all the other teams to feel better because 'they're the problem'. See the vignette, 'Management development with a "dysfunctional" group' in Chapter 10.

How should the coach work with connectedness? Our task is to make the group safe enough for people to form their own connections, and occasionally to reinforce these by commenting on connections that are made. We also need to attend to the obstacles to connectedness, such as unspoken or unrecognized envy or animosity. Hostility is not in itself the enemy of connectedness; *unspoken* hostility is – see 'Competition, envy and admiration' below. In an intact team or between teams, this kind of barrier may have a long history, rendering the coach's task more difficult and complex. If however we can help a team achieve genuine safety for exchange where it has long been lacking, the relief at discussing the undiscussables is great and creates the possibility of a better resolution.[65]

Interpersonal learning

Group coaching can offer opportunities for interpersonal learning that cannot be equalled in any other modality. The range of available interpersonal opportunities are multiplied, both for participation and for observation.

Members can gain a more objective perspective on how they are seen by others through the multiple lenses available for reflection. By becoming more aware of their behaviour, they can begin to understand their own patterns of behaviour in relating to others – for instance that they wait passively for others' attention, or relentlessly seek attention, relate only to some kinds of people, seek approval, or unremittingly compete. They can also observe and digest both similar and contrasting interpersonal styles, opening up a broader range of alternatives understood, through the medium of the group, with head, heart and gut. The process of giving and receiving feedback, and surviving doing so, in itself develops courage and the willingness to take risks.

Vignette: Gender relations

Through feedback in team coaching, Peter realized that he mostly talked to the other men in the group, and when he did speak to female colleagues, tended not to make eye contact.

ALISON: Peter, I can't help noticing that you speak to Mark and Darren a lot of the time.

CAROLINE: The people that really matter – the ones with the dangly bits!

PETER: No –

MARY: I don't think that –

PETER: It's the other way round!

COACH: How do you mean?

PETER: The really important people here are the ones *without* the dangly bits!

COACH: Hmmm? [*with a quizzical expression*]

Peter went on to explain that he was afraid of 'getting it wrong' with women, especially with Alison, the team leader. He added that the women in the team had the real power, and he needed to 'watch his step' to feel secure. Some of the team's forthright women initially derided this feeling, but the two other men in the team acknowledged that they sometimes felt that way too.

The team's work was to provide services to women, and most of its members were women. There had been an unspoken and unchallenged assumption that the women in the team would always 'know best'. The naming and loosening of this assumption helped not only Peter but the whole team to be more open-minded and effective.

Privately Peter told the (female) coach that he had never been comfortable in groups of women after a single-sex education up to university. Airing his feelings helped Peter relax more with his female colleagues, and also surfaced a gender dynamic in the team.

Competition, envy and admiration

We have already noted that comparison and competitiveness can be found in every group. Closely linked to these are envy and admiration, two emotions stirred up when we think that someone is in some way 'better' than we are, or has something that we do not. They are two sides of the same coin. Envy, though, is a horrible feeling, a destructive emotion often pushed below the level of conscious awareness, because feeling it is so hard to bear. Envy can lead us to attack the person who has what we want, for having it. In a group this can be through subtle undermining or more overt 'putting down', or shunning; envy can be very destructive if unchallenged. Envy handled well becomes admiration, and can be transformative.

Admiration is the kinder sister of envy, but it requires a person to recognize her/his envy, and to tolerate having that feeling. We have to bear someone else being smarter, kinder, more courageous, more rigorous or more successful than we are, or having something we don't. When we admire someone, we appreciate the quality, and acknowledge that we would like it for ourselves. This can lead us to emulate the behaviour we admire, and so come to have some of it. From earliest youth, human learning is imitative. Admiration requires us to have the humility to learn, including from those we would prefer to have nothing to teach *us*.

The door is open to envy in any group interaction, through the constant non-conscious process of mutual comparison. Do we fit in? Do we fade into the background well enough/too well? Are we better than/worse than her/him (repeat around the group)? Where are we in the pecking order? We may be more or less conscious of such comparisons. In many people they are so automatic that they have become 'non-conscious', or so unwanted that they have become unconscious.

Making these comparisons with others is a competitive process, and is more or less universal, even if we do not think of ourselves as especially competitive. In many work contexts this is quite evident, though it is usually easier to spot other people's competitiveness than our own. If Jeremy or

Vignette: Envy as an obstacle to collaboration

In the corporate design department, Emma was always sniping at Deirdre. At times she realized she was doing it, but that didn't help her stop. The two were technically on the same level, but Deirdre's creativity meant that she was often the one that other departments sought out. The rest of the team did their best to ignore the dynamic, but now things had reached such a pitch that something had to be done.

The group coach spoke to each team member separately. Emma identified that she was envious of the attention that Deirdre received and felt that she was left to do more than her share of the legwork. Deirdre was feeling increasingly embattled and was thinking of leaving; she told the coach it reminded her of having been bullied at school.

In the group session, the coach talked about normal feelings of competition and encouraged everyone to identify some characteristic in everyone else that they would like for themselves. Emma was surprised to discover that more than one colleague admired her thoroughness and professionalism. There followed a negotiation about what each person would like more of and less of from each other member of the team. Emma found that most of her colleagues wanted her to stop sniping at Deirdre, and Deirdre found that many wanted her to be better at finishing things.

This initial session cleared the air and normalized competitive feelings; over the next few sessions the team supported Emma and Deirdre in sustaining the improvement, in the broader context of everyone working on their team collaboration skills. As the assignment ended Emma and Deirdre were planning a collaboration on a big new project that required them to combine efforts – Deirdre's flair and Emma's project management.

Jenny is very competitive, I can reassure myself that I am less so. More overtly rivalrous colleagues (or friends) make it easier to avoid recognizing our own competitiveness, but that also makes it harder for us as individuals to deal well with envy and succeed through using admiration to motivate ourselves.

As the group coach it is important to be on the alert for these processes, which crop up regularly in any group. Our task is to help group members become aware of their competitive feelings, to 'normalize' them by acknowledging their universality, and to promote emulation rather than attack.

Idealization and emulation

In 'Connectedness and belonging' above we touched on the temporary idealization of the group that gets things going on the best footing; as a group continues to develop, or as a team matures, members gradually acquire a more realistic assessment. There is also the possibility of idealization of one member, or perhaps the group coach, as embodying all the necessary capacities and skills. This is especially common in new groups. When extreme, or persistent, it can be a barrier to learning. If the underlying message is 'if only I could be like you (but I never could be)', there is little room for ordinary admiration, emulation and learning.

The idealization needs to be relinquished, often first in favour of an idealization of the group itself and eventually, a more realistic assessment (see also 'Connectedness and belonging' above). The group coach must encourage this. Curiosity is our friend here. What do group members get out of idealizing someone else? For instance, does it let them off their responsibility to learn? Or fend off a change that no one wants to face?

Ordinary admiration (as opposed to idealization) allows us to explore the quality we admire and understand it more fully. It becomes possible to 'try it on' for ourselves. We can mimic behaviour and find it changes our attitude, or we can achieve a questioning stance to our own previous attitudes, and 'try out' something new. Learning may start with either.

We need not choose between changing attitude and changing behaviour. A permanent change requires both, and something more. It requires that the new behaviour become habitual.

Sometimes emulation will be very subtle and hardly conscious at all, as one member witnesses the success another achieves and begins, non-consciously, to emulate it; articulation comes much later, if at all.

Vignette: Learning the art of influence

David began in the learning group frustrated at why he found it so difficult to influence his team members. He was direct and clear in his instructions; what was so hard for them to understand?

Over a year in the group, he heard other members describe and refine their ways of influencing colleagues, and observed in the group itself how other members tailored their questioning of each other carefully to each individual. He began to experiment with this for himself, first inside, and then outside the group, achieving better results. He later commented that he had been trying to manage his team as though they were machines, and identical ones at that. The practice of other group members had challenged him at least as much as their questions.

David began to think about the individuals he managed and the different approaches they needed from him. As time went on, he began to incorporate these insights into the explicit change strategies he crafted and refined in the group.

Practising courage and freedom to act

Research suggests that people who are active in a group tend both to be most popular or influential and to get the most benefit from group involvement.[66] In part this is related to the development of courage.

Being and speaking openly in a group requires courage. Doing so repeatedly over time develops courage, so that members become freer, requiring less courage in taking smaller risks, and becoming more willing to take larger risks which again require more courage. This development of greater courage and freedom to act in the group can lead to members over time choosing to behave more courageously in other settings. As they bring their experiences back to the group the learning is again reinforced. The greater freedom to act is an important and unsung benefit of group membership.

Vignette: Developing courage

Gilbert was a painfully shy team member. The group coach adopted a forthright yet respectful approach to him, for example asking him, after significant eye contact during periods of Gilbert's silence, 'are you willing to be pressed to contribute today?'. This established a dialogue about Gilbert's lack of verbal contribution; as he did begin to speak occasionally, it became clear that his lack of speech did not reflect lack of engagement: he contributed ideas that had been thought out in depth.

Witnessing and being witnessed

Saying things out loud to another person, things that we have previously only said in our heads, is powerful in itself; it is more powerful in a group of witnesses. We may surprise ourselves with the insights we express, or say more than we intend so that others can mirror back to us things that we had hitherto ignored.

'Did I say that?'

This may impel us to examine things more fully, or to act in a situation where we have previously felt paralysed. This aspect of witnessing is about others witnessing me and my interactions.

On the other side, we have the opportunity to watch as others tell their stories and relate to each other, and can learn through watching what they do and how they do it. For some people, particularly the naturally reflective and the wary, this is a preferred kind of learning. Here is a comment from an action learning set member:

> I learn more from other people's turns than I do from my own because I tend to be more resistant to what people say to me . . . It's seeing how people deal with issues and manage to overcome them – everyone in the set – even though they all come from different angles, are very experienced and have lots of skills – always approached things from a point of view where they didn't feel able to do it, or there was some kind of thing stopping them and seeing how they managed to overcome those issues in order to be able to move forward, was really useful.

Witnessing is a means by which group members gain *information*, an important way in which group life promotes learning. This is information at every level, from quite practical data to profound and partly non-conscious understanding of differences in approach, perhaps for the first time.

Encouragement

Encouragement is both non-verbal and verbal. Where a change has to be made, being in a group and seeing other people make changes is a great encouragement and spur, including for those who are still wavering: it engages competitiveness in a positive way.

Where a positive change is made, it will also be seen and commented on by other group members. Nor should the group coach be above occasionally commenting on positive changes made by individuals, particularly those that no one else has yet highlighted. There is a line to tread here: the group coach's praise is likely to be experienced as particularly powerful by group members, and this useful tool should neither be neglected nor diluted by over-use. Over-use to a particular individual also poses a risk of inciting envy in other group members.

If verbal encouragement is over-used, an over-positive tone can result in the group. What, I hear some readers ask, could possibly be wrong with that? Well yes, there are some problems. The group's capacity for holding contradictory ideas alongside each other – negative and positive feelings about the same thing – is a strength of group coaching, because it reflects the conflicting feelings most of us have even about desired changes. Ask anyone who has ever tried a diet to lose weight!

Vignette: What is most encouraging?

The corporate culture change group had some members going from strength to strength. Every meeting was filled with examples of negatives turned to positives, or of great strides forward in different divisions. As the tone became more and more evangelical, some members became more and more silent, and the atmosphere increasingly tense.

COACH: What isn't being said?

John took a deep breath.

JOHN: I find it impossible to relate to what is being said. In my division, it has been nothing like that. My staff want nothing to do with the programme, and fight me on everything. I've tried being positive – it isn't working!

MEREDITH: Thank God someone has said it. I feel just the same.

JOHN: I felt couldn't talk about it here before – everyone else was doing so well – but my mentor said I should.

JENNY: In my division . . .

Various group members talked about difficulties, resistance and setbacks in an atmosphere of increasing openness and warmth. It was as though the group breathed a collective sigh of relief. Those who had previously spoken only of triumphs now revealed real challenges.

> *COACH:*   What will help us tackle these barriers?
> *MANDY:*   Just being able to tell it like it is is a huge relief – I feel supported.
> *JOHN:*   I guess our staff might feel like that too!
> *MARCO:*   Can I ask you, Bill . . .
>
> The group then turned to planning how to work with their most urgent and important frustrations, agreeing to reconvene in a week to compare notes and refine strategies.

John's courageous action in speaking of failure encouraged and heartened the group, and moved communication to a more realistic and valuable level. This was a quantum leap in the value of the group in driving the change forward.

In the next chapter we look at systems theory, which offers an explanation about how the assertion of any value is inevitably balanced by its opposite (see 'The necessity of paradox'). If the downside is systematically excluded from discussion, the resulting feeling of unreality impedes progress. The coach's role was simply to raise the possibility of another view, and after exploration, steer the group back to its primary task in the light of the fuller information now available.

Group performance coaching

At times group members will focus on a dilemma faced by a particular member, and will offer feedback and advice on how to handle it from several different viewpoints. Often then the member will report back on progress, or the group will 'check in' to see how it went. Further shared reflection may then illuminate the next steps. There is no need for the coach to take a very active role in any of this, unless s/he thinks that an important angle has been overlooked. In a group, members can benefit as much from the confidence-enhancing experience of helping others as from being helped. The group process naturally reinforces the interdependence that is our true state – sometimes helping, sometimes needing help.

This kind of behaviour is self-reinforcing. The more members bring their dilemmas for the group's coaching, and the more successes the group experiences in the coaching role, the more they will bring more, in a virtuous cycle.

There are two potential problems here, for which the group coach must be alert. The first is that a particular member will always or mostly be the person coached. This kind of unequal interaction usually indicates that group members are avoiding something – perhaps the areas where they feel less competent or more vulnerable – which the 'always coached' member expresses on their behalf. If it persists, this pattern will damage the group and reduce its task effectiveness, because the thing avoided is likely to be the challenge members most need to face. The group coach should highlight the pattern, and freely express her/his curiosity about its significance, including what it is that everyone else gets out of being so helpful to Charlie all the time.

The second problem is when one or more of the members is particularly persistent in pushing a particular viewpoint as holding 'the answer' to the other member's problems. The insistence is the clue here. The group coach should direct her/his curiosity to why the advice-giver is so insistent – does the situation under discussion echo something in their own experience? What has led them to be so involved with Charlie's dilemma? Could it be that there is an echo of some dilemma of their own?

The roles of the group coach

Considering everything covered in Part 2, it seems that the group coach needs sophisticated skills. Further, group coaching done well is unobtrusive, practically invisible.

Research found 'skilled, knowledgeable, psychologically informed, flexible and resilient facilitation' to be one of the two most important factors in learning[67] groups, the other being a sense of psychological safety, the 'holding' described in Chapter 2. Though unobtrusive, the group coach's role is important.

There are five important dimensions to the group coach's role of holding (see 'Holding' in Chapter 2): protecting the boundaries of the group, studying the group's interactions, representing authority or experience in the group, limiting scapegoating and other destructive behaviour, and attending to the group's system administration.

Boundary keeper

The group coach keeps the group focused on its task, makes sure that it starts and finishes on time, refocuses the group on agreed goals, tests relevance, and deals with interruptions to the work. See also 'What enables the group coach to hold a group effectively?' in Chapter 2.

The coach is guardian of the group's way of working. This is complex, because s/he is also educating the group in how to work more effectively, so that the modus operandi is in a constant process of negotiation and change.

Student of the group's interactions

The group coach must help the group's work by reinforcing behaviour that promotes learning, and and commenting on barriers to effective working. It is often helpful to offer ideas for group members' evaluation, so that they are invited to work with us in understanding how the group's dynamics help it to achieve its purposes, or hinder it. The process is one of exploring together so as to understand more fully.

Some of the interventions we may use are highlighting issues, confronting or pointing out particular behaviour, underlining certain contributions, clarifying what has been said, and acknowledging and receiving others' contributions. These also model the kinds of behaviour we want to see between group members. See 'Working together effectively' (text box) in Chapter 9, and 'Beginnings, middles and endings of sessions' in Chapter 11.

Representing authority/experience in the group

When anxiety is high, group members exert pressure on the group coach to 'lead' them. While the group coach does not fully embrace this role, s/he may become more active in the group, so that members can rediscover their own authority, experience and strength. This doesn't necessarily mean becoming the 'leader' – it might involve calmly asking the members more questions, for instance. It reduces anxiety to the point where members can think, and act, again, and the group can return to 'normal'. The leadership role can again be relinquished.

Limiting scapegoating and other destructive behaviour

When the group is behaving destructively, for example scapegoating a particular member, the coach's role is to act to prevent or reduce further destructiveness. See also 'What enables the group coach to hold a group effectively?' in Chapter 2, and 'Location' in Chapter 3.

With scapegoating, the first step is to identify the process with words, and help the group understand why they need a scapegoat; it is likely to be related to a wider anxiety. If it persists, the coach must ally herself/himself with the scapegoat and continue to challenge the group to achieve understanding of the process.

System administrator

- Preparing the setting – seats, table, colleagues who need to be informed.
- Considering the host institution, its impact on the group and the group's impact on it.
- Preparing the group members – individual meetings before the group begins.
- Preserving the boundaries of the group – group room, timing, timescale, privacy.
- Monitoring communication into and out of the group – messages, extra-group communication.

System administration is discussed further in Chapter 11.

What are the characteristics of an effective group coach?

The group coach must be able to tolerate anxiety even at high levels, and think on her/his feet under pressure. S/he intervenes courageously when needed, and refrains from acting when that is needed. S/he accepts her own and her clients' limitations while retaining the hope of improvement.

The effective group coach needs:

- business wisdom and personal wisdom
- self-knowledge
- psychological insight
- group experience as a member
- curiosity and warmth towards others
- training and experience in working with groups
- continuous professional development
- supervision from someone with group expertise
- a sense of professional ethics guiding her/his work
- sufficient consonance of values with the values of the client organization.

The team coach also needs:

- the ability to tolerate and work with powerful feelings and projections, including negative ones
- an ability to learn and temporarily inhabit the team's world/context
- the tact and resilience to forge an effective working alliance with the team's leader
- the ability to tolerate and work creatively with the ambiguities of her/his role *vis-à-vis* the leader, the team, the organization and the task.

Not all group coaching assignments are equally complex in terms of the demands on the coach. Interventions with an intact team require more, particularly if it is a senior team with broad organizational responsibilities.

Finally: Concluding Part 2

In conclusion, the core processes in individual and group learning are holding and exchange, and the nine group processes described in Chapter 3 underlie all group interactions. The eight further factors described in this chapter relate to promoting effective learning in groups. The discovery of these processes has been through practice, and practice continues to define them more precisely. Over 50 years ago Kurt Lewin[68] pointed out the inextricability of theory and practice in group dynamics, and the potential for group theory to offer highly practical solutions. In this spirit, these summaries of group theory are offered to group coaches for use and discussion.

In the next chapter we shift our focus to the context of group coaching, the broader organization. As you read the rest of the book, look for the processes from these three chapters operating in the stories in the book, and in your own memories stirred by what you read.

Part 3

Understanding organizations, groups and teams: systems thinking

This chapter

In order to coach any group or team effectively, and particularly a senior team, we need an understanding of its context in an organization. Modern organizational life is multi-layered, and the group coach must be able to think about many layers of a 'system' (see below) relating simultaneously. This chapter links the previous chapters about interpersonal processes in groups with the broader context of organizational life. What we do as group coaches with one part of an organization will affect, and be affected by, what happens in all the other parts. Many group coaching assignments are indeed part of a broader programme for change in the company, of which the coach needs awareness and understanding.

This chapter contains:
- This chapter
- Systems thinking: an outline
- Systems and teams
- Where is the boundary of the system?
- How does change happen?
- The necessity of paradox
- Working with systems thinking
- Working with complexity
- Working with more than one part of the system
- Groups and decision-making
- Influencing change in organizations
- Large groups
- Working with large groups: de Maré and dialogue
- Restructuring the large group into smaller groups
- World café
- Open space technology (OST)
- Finally

This chapter offers a broad introduction to systems theory as it applies to organizations. Systems theory is a way of thinking that helps us to reflect on the complexities of modern organizational life. The chapter offers a kind of 'whistle-stop tour', summarizing a range of systems-related theoretical approaches to organizations, including complexity and chaos theory. It also offers a brief look at decision-making in groups, including 'groupthink', the process through which groups make poor decisions through a lack of robust disagreement and dialogue. Those already conversant with a systems approach will find the material familiar, while the bibliography at the end of the book offers some leads for those who would like to pursue these ideas further. For the business professional, this chapter can shed some light on how effective group coaching can improve business performance.

Systems theory comes from a different strand of scientific tradition to the group dynamics theory described in the last three chapters, but it is part of the same scientific paradigm, and linked in another important way. The interpersonal processes observed at small group level have been found to account for learning phenomena observed in large organizations; research has found causal links between interpersonal enquiry, interactions between different parts of the system, and learning characteristics of whole organizations.[69] See also 'Groups and decision-making' below. As you read on, have in mind the group processes described in Part 2, and consider how they contribute to the vignettes in the book, and to your own experiences that the book brings to mind.

The chapter also touches briefly on some methods of working at inter-group level and in larger groups. Though not strictly coaching interventions, since they address individual needs only incidentally, these are relevant to coaches asked to design or deliver broader organizational interventions, particularly when working with senior teams with strategic responsibilities.

Systems thinking: an outline

'Systems' is a way of thinking that seeks to engage with the complexity of reality, including the dynamics of shifts through time. In origin, systems theory is a biological model,[70] a meta-theory or framework for learning derived in many fields. The description in this chapter is necessarily a simplification; systems theory itself, however, teaches us that without some simplification we are paralysed by the complexity of reality.

As companies have developed greater precision and efficiency in industrial, technological and management processes in order to compete, these processes have become more complex. In order to avoid being overwhelmed by complexity, it became essential to develop a way of thinking about complexity. Systems theory was the result, bringing together discoveries and epistemologies from many fields.

Systems thinking is a discipline for seeing wholes. It is a framework for seeing inter-relationships rather than things, for seeing patterns of change rather than static 'snapshots'.[71] It offers a more accurate way of understanding the whole field, including apparently unrelated pieces of information, and avoiding misattribution of cause and effect. It produces better action based on that understanding.[72] We can also distinguish between detail complexity – the large number of variables that may weigh on a decision – and dynamic complexity, the attempt to understand the often subtle links between cause and effect through time.[73]

Thinking of organizations as living systems, or organisms, has major benefits: it raises questions about the organization's relationship to its environment, including other organizations, and challenges mechanistic management approaches, wholly inadequate in twenty-first-century economies, moving our thinking towards a more pluralistic approach.[74]

Systems thinking has proven particularly effective with:

- problems whose solutions are not obvious
- complex problems that involve helping many actors see the 'big picture' and not just their part of it
- recurring problems or those made worse by past attempts to fix them
- issues where an action affects or is affected by the environment surrounding the issue.

Systems and teams

Teams are social systems, or subsystems of larger systems (depending on your focus). The concept of 'nested systems' is helpful here. Most systems contain nested systems; that is, subsystems within the system. A team can be thought of as a 'nested system' or subsystem of a larger system, the department or the organization. Similarly, a team's members can be seen as 'nested systems' of the team – subsystems that are grouped together within the system.

It is at our peril that we ignore the system within which our client team or group operates. Nevertheless, it is a practical starting point to focus on the part of the system with which we have been invited to work, the group or team.

Teams are affected by all changes in connected systems or in the system as a whole, but are *not* equally affected by all changes. A team-system interacts with other systems, exchanging information, known as *feedback*. Where things stay within broadly normal parameters, the feedback serves to adjust the system's functioning. Managing the flow of information into and out of the team-system is a critical factor in the health of a system.[75] The diagram opposite shows in simple form the many layers moving outwards from a team.

For example, in working with a team, its members are subsystems interacting with each other. At the very least, the group coach must pay attention to the team as a whole and to each of its members. Each team member also interacts

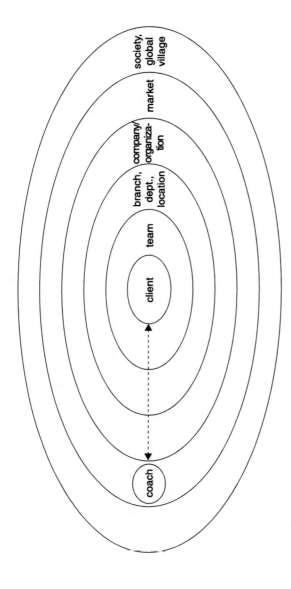

The context of coaching

horizontally with other teams within the organization, and with other contacts outside the organization. The team members interact vertically with the team leader, who may also be part of another team, and with the leaders of teams that report to them. In addition, team members each have their own 'ecology', with internal forces at play, and more personal external links.

Sometimes it becomes clear in our work that the problem we are addressing cannot be wholly solved in the part of the organization's system with which we are working.

Vignette: A change ordered by HQ

The UK managers of a global motor business are charged with conveying to staff the company's unpalatable global message that only those whose performance is outstanding will receive a pay rise in future. This is part of a new 'aggressive performance management strategy'. Local managers receive furious and/or incredulous responses from their staff, and the company's response is to offer the managers coaching in 'dealing with difficult people'. A further complexity is that the news is received in different ways in the 60 countries in which the company operates. The coach helps the managers articulate their own reactions to the news, and to develop their ability to tell people difficult facts. He also facilitates a discussion about whether they wish to comment to HQ on the policy and its effects in the UK.

At a psychological level, money most often equates to value; 'if I am not worth even an inflation increase, then the company doesn't value me very much'. The hard facts of the situation and accompanying resentment remain, and managers will have to work harder than before to help the 'good' and 'good enough' majority maintain motivation. Because the UK team concludes that it cannot change the policy itself, the coaching is an exercise in damage limitation.

Where is the boundary of the system?

In contracting for an assignment, the team coach needs some definition of the boundary of the team. When thinking about organizations, groups and teams, however, the definition of the boundary of the system is somewhat arbitrary. For example, in working with senior management teams (SMTs), is the system this team, or the company as a whole? All systems are like Russian dolls, or perhaps like mirror reflections of mirrors, stretching away into infinity. There is a risk here of being overwhelmed by complexity, particularly now that modern information technology can give us a clearer sense of its scale.[76] The concept of nested systems helps us find our way through these complexities, and locate the boundary where it is most usefully drawn.

The systems map overleaf is not complete – it could go on and on. In working with a company's most senior team, there is always an ambiguity about the extent of the system. Since the team is also responsible for the strategic direction of the company, everything relevant to that affects its task. Time, especially the future, is also a factor. How long is the current way of working going to keep the company profitable? What changes would it have to make to secure profitability for the next five years? Like the typewriter manufacturers of old, will a time come when, if they do not redefine their identity and/or focus, their product and so their company will become obsolete? How responsive to change has the company been up to now, and what are its characteristics that will improve the chances of adapting successfully to future market changes?

Systems thinking in management has been influenced by new scientific ideas in physics and biology, as well as ecology and anthropology,[77] greatly enhancing its ability to engage with complexity. If the universe is one whole, with constant change as a given,[78] where does the system start, and end? And if all management is now the management of change, what understanding of change do coaches need in order to prepare their clients for the complexity of twenty-first-century management?

Deckchair company senior management team interrelationships

How does change happen?

The butterfly effect

In a famous example of the interconnection of causality, the butterfly moving its wings in Beijing sets off a chain of events causing tropical storms in the Gulf of Mexico. It is not the butterfly that causes the weather change. It triggers a small change, which triggers another, and another ... which may trigger another that happens to be a critical random factor 'tipping' the weather towards a different pattern.

Chaos theory and complexity theory have together led to important advances in our understanding of how change occurs. Complex systems are characterized by multiple patterns of interaction that may be ordered or chaotic. Chaos theory has demonstrated repeatedly that order, in the form of pattern, always emerges from randomness and apparent chaos if a sufficiently large system is observed.

Migrating birds flock and fly together without colliding for great distances; the ants in an anthill cooperate towards shared purposes;[79] people on a New York pavement weave around each other in complex patterns requiring sophisticated coordination skills.[80] Evidence of innate self-organizing capacities can be found across the animal kingdom, including humans. James Surowiecki goes further, and argues convincingly that large numbers of independent thinkers whose views are aggregated and averaged can be depended upon for accurate judgement and prediction[81] (see further 'Groups and decision-making' below).

These pattern-forming self-organizing processes can become a resource for managing change, and some newer methods of working with larger groups of people, such as world café and open space technology, are based on their capacity to allow a new 'order' to emerge. See 'World café' and 'Open space technology' below.

Chaos scientists have studied the way in which these

patterns emerge under the influence of competing 'attractors', tending to stabilize or destabilize the system. This is not a smooth process. Many incremental shifts can move the system from equilibrium to an unstable 'edge of chaos' where the possibility exists of the system 'flipping' into an entirely new pattern, as with the butterfly and the weather system. The response of the system to these random factors will always be to self-organize around the new pattern, creating a new state of equilibrium – for a while. Clearly this is a long way from the old certainties that a particular action might predictably produce a particular result.

Managers, encouraged by their coaches, must become adept in using small shifts to create a climate in which change is likely to occur. The emphasis shifts from power to influence. Every initiative is an experiment, the results of which can be used to refine the next move. All failures, total or partial, provide information. Senior managers must give up the illusion of control in favour of the real possibility of influence, so as to craft more subtle interventions with a higher chance of positive outcomes.

How does group coaching fit into this picture? Well, coaching groups offer a 'bounded instability'[82] within which anxiety can be transformed into a source of creativity, through communication and dialogue. It reproduces the 'edge of chaos' conditions in which change can occur and offers managers the opportunity to study and work in real time with the forces of change. See the vignette, 'Median reflection group in the aftermath of war' below.

These discoveries also make sense of the importance of the informal communication processes in and between groups in all organizations. These exchanges are the medium of culture, the glue that holds the company together or that which deepens its fragmentation. Attempts to suppress informal communication always fail: far better to work to influence them.

The necessity of paradox

The final aspect of systems thinking that we will consider is the necessity of living with paradox. When we try to change something, we run into resistance in the status quo.[83] Consider the many organizational change programmes that fail (see the Preface). Every position tends to generate its opposite. One common but ineffective way of living with paradox is to have an 'espoused theory' (the one that everyone acknowledges as the goal) and a 'theory-in-use' (the one that actually guides action[84]). There is more about how to work with this kind of problem in 'Working with unconscious and unspoken conflicts' (Chapter 10).

Although paradoxes can paralyse, they can also be levers for change. Organizations' paradoxical expectations (see box below) often have merit on both sides. Paradoxes cannot truly be resolved, because of the inherent tendency of a position to generate its own opposite.

The organization's paradoxical requirements[85]

Innovate	↔	avoid mistakes
Think long-term	↔	deliver results now
Cut costs	↔	increase morale
Reduce staff	↔	improve teamwork
Be flexible	↔	respect the rules
Collaborate	↔	compete
Decentralize	↔	retain control
Specialize	↔	be opportunistic
Low costs	↔	high quality

Groups are good at holding and surfacing paradox. The group coach's role is to help group members recognize the paradoxical positions they hold and make sense of the tension, and help them resist coming down on one side or the other. Instead, the tensions between the two sides of the paradox must be held so that the benefits of both can be gained. The paradox is not 'resolved' but exploited.

For example, devolving power within explicit limits, such as cost ceilings or value/goal statements, can release creativity without generating pandemonium; to encourage learning from mistakes (experience) through cross-departmental reflective groups, such as action learning sets, can seed a culture change towards thoughtful innovation. In the last decades of the twentieth century, Japan led the world in reducing costs while increasing quality through improving design and so simplifying production.

For the group coach, holding the possibility that several apparently contradictory views of an issue have merit is a core skill. In groups, the richness of paradox can contribute to genuinely innovative solutions to pressing business problems.

A group coach asking the apparently simple question 'what isn't being said?' can bring forth a range of response contradicting the ostensible harmony of moments before; yet the group can then 'hold' and make sense of these multiple viewpoints, evincing a more rounded and complex view of current reality. See the vignette, 'Reflection process 1' in Chapter 8.

Working with systems thinking

Systems thinking about organizations helps make sense of experience, but at the same time clarifies the profound challenges posed to individuals working in modern organizations. A very great deal of our work as coaches is about helping individuals adjust to, and operate skilfully within, the dynamic complexity of modern business life. In order to help people thrive while living with the reality of constant change, we need paradoxically to make as certain and stable as possible those things that are under our control. We provide the 'holding' that enables something new to be truly taken on, and enable our clients to do the same for their staff.

Groups excel at this, because we are inherently social and have always lived in groups that succeeded through our collective ability to adapt. 'The human individual is a political animal and cannot find fulfilment outside a group, and cannot satisfy any emotional drive without expression of its social component.'[86] For most people, membership in a group seems in itself to satisfy deeply felt needs and so offer enough stability to encounter and master change. What is shared is normalized (see further 'Connectedness and belonging' and 'The roles of the group coach' in Chapter 4), reducing panic and enabling thought and action.

Working with complexity

How else can systems thinking help us in our work as coaches? In at least two ways. First, by giving us a framework for understanding the complex task of modern leadership, and so understanding the nature of the executive role more fully. The box shows five challenges for modern managers that are also opportunities with which their coaches can help.

Guidelines for managing complexity[87]

- Rethink what we mean by organization, especially the nature of hierarchy and control
- Learn the art of managing and changing contexts
- Learn how to use small changes to create large effects
- Live with continuous transformation and emergent order as a natural state of affairs
- Be open to new metaphors that can facilitate processes of self-organization.

Everything is temporary: business leaders, and their coaches, must see existing hierarchies as provisional and become skilled at analysing their present and predicted usefulness to goals. The executive's role shifts from managing structures to managing contexts that allow functional forms of self-organization to occur.

Second, systems thinking makes it clear that it is essential to think on many levels at once about our work. Looking again at the map of coaching work on page 91, we can understand the client's situation as fully as possible: the coach needs to think about every level of their context.

This chapter is focused on the context within which groups and teams operate, but the coach must also attend to the individuals within each team, and to the other systems touching them . . . the value of a theory of dynamics and complexity becomes more and more evident. As a focus, the group or team is serviceably close to the midpoint of the system map, allowing the focus to move at times towards the individual and at times towards the organizational and broader context: a practical position for the solving of problems. Further, this can be a tool for evaluating our coaching. If everything is interconnected, what is the observable impact of our coaching interventions? The coach too is a part of the system.

Coaches working with systems thinking: chaos and complexity

- Everything is interconnected: keep the whole picture in mind
- What are the leveraging small actions that will help this group to shift?
- You need both horns of the dilemma: challenge the 'resolution' of paradox
- Pay attention to the quality of interfaces and communications between different parts of the system.

Working with more than one part of the system

At times our team coaching work highlights the need for the team to interact more productively with another team within the system. The vignette illustrates an intervention aimed at improving communication between a senior team and its board.

Vignette: Inter-team communication

While coaching the senior management team of a not-for-profit pressure group, it became clear that many of the problems arose through a poor communication with the Board, some of whom were prone to interfere in operational decisions. There was mistrust on both sides, sometimes obstructing the organization's effectiveness.

The coach convened a Board/SMT day focusing on roles and responsibilities. Throughout the day, small groups were explicitly mixed in membership between the two 'teams', Board and SMT. It opened with small groups where individuals shared the stories of their involvement in the cause, and then, first in small groups and subsequently in the whole group (eighteen people), some exercises focusing on the overarching goals and values of the organization. These exercises reaffirmed that all present shared values and common goals, a spur making better collaboration both essential and more achievable.

The two 'teams' then convened separately, to list on flipcharts what they needed from the other group, and what they could offer the other group. The flipcharts were then 'paired', needs of one to the offers of the other, and vice versa. This exercise focused each group on its role and responsibilities in relation to the organization's goals, and facilitated a negotiation in plenary between the two groups where a greater degree of mutual understanding was achieved. Arrangements were agreed for taking the collaboration arrangements forward, and reviewing them after a six-month period.

What is ostensibly happening here is a focus on roles and responsibilities – pretty standard stuff for a team coach. At a more profound level participants find commonality, a kind of organizational 'holding' (see 'Connectedness and belonging' in Chapter 4), in exchanging information about their commitment to the cause. They are subtly reminded (through the exercises) that the cause is more important than smaller agendas, and invited to reexamine behaviour as well as roles through the open language of 'need and offer'. The cause itself challenges the petty behaviour that had been hampering progress. The design allows agreements about desired behaviour to be secured without post-mortem or recrimination.

The six-month review, however, is a critical component. Without this, it is likely that over time bad habits will reassert themselves.

Especially in larger organizations, difficulties between teams or departments cause as many problems as difficulties within a particular team. At times it can seem that something tribal in us is activated, and vicious rivalries can develop. See 'Connectedness and belonging' and 'Competition, envy and admiration' in Chapter 4, and 'Bion: a theory of group dysfunction' and 'Teams declared dysfunctional' in Chapter 10.

Working with more than one part of the system is complicated, particularly over time; the coach runs various risks, including that of being seen as aligned with one or another part of the system. Accepting this risk and incorporating it into the design can be a creative solution, as in this example.

Vignette: Cross-national team dynamics

Jean-Luc, a French coach hired to work with the French-based senior management team and US-based global marketing team of an upscale cosmetics company, approached an American colleague, Wendell, to co-facilitate the work. The total number of people in the two teams was about fourteen, so having two coaches enabled attention to each individual and in particular to the CEO who had commissioned the work.

The two teams had been at loggerheads for some time. The US team was extremely concerned about the future viability of the business in the face of stiff international competition; they believed that the mother company in France was complacent. The French team believed that the US team was alarmist, and that the business would survive because of the innovative science that had so far given them the edge.

The conflict between the two teams became enacted in the relationship between Jean-Luc and Wendell as they planned the initial coaching event, with Wendell wanting to simplify the initial design radically. Jean-Luc at last agreed to a simplified programme.

The opening event succeeded in refocusing the two teams round their shared goals, and for the first time the French team acknowledged the hard business realities emphasized by the US team. Everyone felt that their voice was heard. A tentative accord was reached about the company's next steps, including continuing to be coached together in the interests of the company as a whole.

Having a French and an American coach bridged the differences and allowed all those present to feel that their interests were represented in the planning and process of the coaching event. Jean-Luc's comment afterwards that the original design would not have succeeded mirrored the acceptance of the US data by the French team.

Coaching groups mixing members of teams from different countries are useful for cross-cultural education and increasing cultural sensitivity,[88] and can improve the quality of corporate decision-making.

Groups and decision-making

It is 'a truth universally acknowledged' that groups make better-quality decisions than individuals. But is it true?

James Surowiecki's fascinating book *The wisdom of crowds*[89] assembles a compelling mass of evidence that the aggregated judgements of large numbers of people will reliably outperform the judgement of individuals, however expert the individuals or inexpert the group members. It seems that the averaging process reconciles the diverse and cancels out the idiosyncratic, homing in on the 'best guess' with a remarkable degree of accuracy. The interconnected factors crucial to a group's ability to arrive at good-quality decisions are: decentralization, which promotes diversity, local knowledge and independence of view, and the use of private or specialist knowledge; and some mechanism for aggregating all the independent views. Intriguingly, Surowiecki argues among other things for utilizing this collective wisdom through betting markets, where those 'voting' never meet each other.

So how is it that many work teams and other small groups regularly perform at the effectiveness level of their least effective members? How does 'groupthink', the ability of small groups to stifle dissent and ignore important relevant information, come to hold such sway?

Research has demonstrated that in groups where different views are not present (because we have appointed 'people like us'), or are suppressed out of fear or exaggerated respect for authority, 'groupthink' will set in, stifle debate and lead to poor-quality decisions. This was famously and tragically demonstrated by the investigation of the NASA Columbia mission.[90] Groupthink is more likely in groups where status is closely linked to group conformity.[91] Its symptoms include collective rationalization to discount information that might lead to questioning or reconsidering; stereotyped views of 'outsiders' who are therefore not consulted; a pressure towards uniformity and self-censorship, giving the illusion of unanimity as the importance of doubts is minimized; and the direct suppression of counter-arguments and those who make them.[92]

Groupthink is most likely to arise in certain circumstances: in highly homogeneous groups as regards social background and ideology; where leaders do not encourage open enquiry and evaluation, or bring in outside views for advice or evaluation; where procedures promoting good decision-making are lacking. A series of studies of American foreign policy in the twentieth century illustrate these points.[93] In these circumstances groups polarize, and tend after deliberation to conclude a more extreme position in line with their existing predilections. Further, extreme views tend to correlate with holding views rigidly, compounding the problem,[94] particularly within homogeneous groups. These are several of the reasons that a positive diversity strategy makes sound business sense.

It is easy to see a link between groupthink and Argyris' work on organizational 'undiscussables' (see Chapter 10).

The role of organizational leaders in setting an example of and promoting a culture of openness and questioning is critical.[95] This does not necessarily imply a facilitative leadership style – strong leaders can use their strength to promote diversity of views and vigorous debate.

The group coach can promote the expression of diverse views to promote the greatest possible range of information being considered in the making of decisions. Over time group coaching can help a work group internalize the habits of dissent and debate that researchers agree to be fundamental to good-quality decision-making. Reflecting together to see all sides of an argument is a skill that can become a habit, and can best be developed together. Effective group coaching helps a team face the 'unthinkable', and use their diverse viewpoints for business advantage. The pros and cons, and the longevity of this style of intervention have also been considered by Argyris (see 'Argyris' theory of organizational defences' in Chapter 10).

Influencing change in organizations

When we speak of changing organizational 'culture', we are referring to changing the 'theory-in-use' (see 'Mr Team' box in Chapter 6) – the attitudes, assumptions and beliefs demonstrated in behaviour – of a 'critical mass' of people, enough sufficiently influential people to seed a new shared 'culture'[96] throughout the enterprise. See the vignette, 'Action learning for culture change through key individuals' in Chapter 4. The director and other leaders of an organization are influential in creating culture (whether they consciously use their influence or not), but there will be others with significant influence – because of expertise, commitment, visibility, long service, popularity or personal charisma.

The group mechanisms explored in Part 2 are the means of 'feedback', communications from one part of the system to another that allow changes to influence the system as a whole. To change an organization, change must take hold among a critical mass of people. Large groups can have a transformative potential reaching many people.

Large groups

Organizations are large groups, sometimes very large ones, where all the individual members never meet face to face, let alone meet face to face all together. Organizations spread over several locations face the problem that most members will identify primarily with those they work near, whom they see regularly, or with whom they work regularly (even if remote). There may be little sense of the company (or even the department) as a whole. Some companies have experimented with large group meetings as a way of encouraging employee involvement. The aim of such groups is mutual understanding and exchange, in dialogue.

Meeting in large groups can stimulate anxiety in individuals, such as fears of attack or of being lost in the crowd. The experience of being in a group of twenty-five is qualitatively different to being in a group of seven; being in a group of 100 is different again. Intimacy is not possible, and the sense of individual identity may be shaken, as we feel the 'pull' to be part of the group.

Although these feelings exist in all groups, they are felt more intensely in larger groups where the group is experienced as stronger in relation to the individual. It follows that the larger the group, the greater the degree of anxiety. (See also 'Anxiety in groups' in Chapter 10.) Members feel fear and hope about the impact of their group membership on their identity as individuals. Will membership of this group make me feel better about myself, or worse? It can be represented as in the box opposite.

In any group, *all* individuals experience the tension between these needs in some form, although at different intensities and in different ways. In larger groups the range of communications at the individual level is more restricted. The increased size of the group increases pressure on individuals, who may respond destructively (see Chapter 10), or by containing the pressure and expressing it, given time and opportunity, through dialogue. The aim of the large group is to achieve dialogue, bringing people together in mutual understanding.

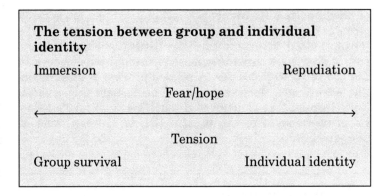

The tension between group and individual identity

Immersion   Repudiation

Fear/hope

←——————————————————————————————→

Tension

Group survival   Individual identity

Working with large groups: de Maré and dialogue

Pat de Maré and his colleagues[97] specialized in the practice
and study of large groups, extending Bion's ideas of frustration leading to thought in the individual (described in
'The development of thinking and obstacles to learning' in
Chapter 2), to the role of frustration in creating dialogue and
culture in larger groups of people. In a larger group various
needs are routinely frustrated: intimacy, recognition, even
a sense of identity may be threatened. These experiences
in the individual can turn either towards destructiveness
or towards a transformative verbal expression that leads in
the group to dialogue. In dialogue, mutual understanding
and 'koinonia', impartial fellowship with others, can be
achieved. The individual who can engage in dialogue gains
more sense of her/his own autonomy and responsibility:

> Now I can see what being a small cog in a big wheel really
> means. I can make choices about whom in the organization
> I confront, and about how I do it.

> It is I who avoid conceptualizing the total department
> because of my catastrophic expectations. In order to
> change the organization I need to attend to my
> department, it will then impact on other departments.[98]

Although in our 'brave new world' the need for dialogue
has never been greater, this method for working with large

or median (ten to twenty-five people) groups, structured only by limits of time and space, is not a venture for the inexperienced or untrained. The institutions listed at the end of this book provide some educational experiences in the use of these processes. A related process, social dreaming, encourages the expression of previously unconscious links through the sharing of dreams.[99] The vignette below gives an example of the uses of the de Maréan style of dialogue group.

Vignette: Median reflection group in the aftermath of war

Shortly after the war in Bosnia, a group analyst worked with a group of leaders from Serbia, Croatia, Albania, Macedonia and other Balkan countries. Each member represented a national organization funding local projects promoting ethnic integration, and wanted to share good practice and develop meaningful ways of evaluating the work through a series of learning conferences.

The group included members from many ethnic, religious and national configurations, some very recently or even currently at war. Despite good intentions, mutual mistrust and fear was never far away. The analyst used action learning and storytelling methodologies with the group, and each day ended with a reflective plenary group without agenda, to allow members' thoughts and learning to emerge, and to develop greater mutual trust and capacity for productive cooperation. The group worked in English, a language of which the group analyst was the only native speaker. At times members from different countries who spoke similar languages would translate for each other.

The space for free dialogue allowed previously hidden hostility and fear to be spoken. The shadow of war was always present: one participant reminded the analyst that relationships could deteriorate as well as improve, even to the point of lethal conflict. As the group worked towards more honest communication, many experienced a new freedom to express their experience.

These gains were always fragile: at different times they were overset by the resurgence of prejudice, by insensitive management of the conferences, by issues of competition and rivalry for limited resources. Nevertheless new links were made, small but genuine steps forward in achieving an atmosphere of equality and mutual respect.

Restructuring the large group into smaller groups

More accessible to most coaches are methods that break larger groups into smaller units, reducing anxiety and allowing each person in the group to contribute. In recent years there have been a couple of interesting developments in this field, 'world café' and 'open space technology', which rely on the propensity of systems to self-organize – see 'The butterfly effect' above. These two variations on a theme are increasingly used in business and community settings. Advice on how to conduct either is readily available on the internet.

World café

World café relies on informal webs of conversation as a means of social learning and meaning-making. In its emphasis on conversations, world café has some commonality with a systems-based style of coaching. The group process allows for cross-fertilization through its fluidity of smaller group membership, and a weaving together of emerging insights from the web of knowledge creation of which smaller conversations are a part.

The physical setting is relaxed, with several small tables as foci for small groups. The larger group gathers around a theme of common concern, and divides randomly into small

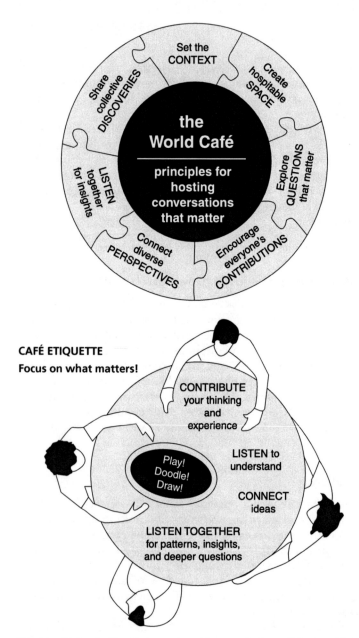

World café: both diagrams reprinted by permission of The World Café Community Foundation.[100]

groups, which gather informally round café style tables. The tables have white paper 'tablecloths' and flipchart pens. Each table focuses on a key question which may be pre-negotiated and written on the 'cloth', or self-generated 'live' in relation to the theme of the event. Learning proceeds through discussion, and key points or images are noted on the 'tablecloths'.

After an agreed period, say 20–60 minutes, all but one member of the informal group move to another table, and the remaining member 'hosts' the discussion for the new group forming at each table. The purpose of this is to cross-fertilize and build on previous conversations. This is repeated three or so times before the whole group is drawn into a plenary to summarize their learning together

World café is a good method for generating ideas and opening up discussion which may allow a consensus view to emerge. Its value is its capacity to hold opposing ideas alongside each other.

Open space technology (OST)

A similar technique, developed by Harrison Owen and colleagues in the mid-1980s, is open space technology (OST). It is a method of working in large groups with devolved leadership, requiring little advance planning but having some prerequisites.

Open space prerequisites

- A compelling theme clearly articulated
- An interested and committed group
- A time and place
- A leader to start things off.

Detailed advance agendas are regarded as unhelpful. Commitment to the full time involved is a part of the contract: the work should not be interrupted, so no drop-ins, and people coming at the start are expected to stay till the end.

Open space framework

- Opening and agenda setting
- Open space
- Conclusion.

Opening

At the beginning of an open space the participants sit in a circle, or in concentric circles for large groups (20 to 1000+ people). In the room there should be a large wall onto which many pieces of paper may be stuck.

The leader greets everyone and briefly states the theme of the gathering. Then all participants are invited to identify any issue or opportunity related to the theme, write it onto a large sheet of paper and post it on the wall. This creates the agenda. No one has to suggest a topic, but if they do, they must care about the issue and join the group discussing it.

Open space

The meeting now organizes itself, and the leader's role is to do as little as possible to get in the way of that. All members are invited to sign up for the sessions that interest them. Since many sessions run concurrently, everyone has to choose the topics that they feel most strongly about. People may switch to another session at any time; participants are encouraged to end any discussion that has ceased to be productive.

Conclusion

A rejoining in plenary to conclude the event, with contributions from members commenting on what has been learned or what action is indicated. The meeting ends on time or when the work is completed, whichever is sooner.

Three examples of open space in action[101]

In 1991, US West used OST for a 3-day, 175-person labour-management summit meeting to resolve escalating contract conflicts, avert a major strike, recover from a damaging flood, and prepare itself for telecom mergers and the buildout of the internet.

In South Africa OST was used to help build community connections and lay the groundwork for cooperative business activities in the midst of post-apartheid confusion. One meeting brought 300 senior transportation executives together. Another gathered 80 community choir leaders.

Rockport Shoes held a 3-day, 300-person company-wide strategy conference in one of its warehouses and stumbled onto a couple of brand new product lines that netted $18 million in their first year of sales. The idea came from the security guard and made the previously quite sceptical CFO very happy.

Open space works best when used to work on something that participants care passionately about and will take responsibility for taking forward; when the issue is complex so that diverse and conflicting viewpoints are a benefit; and when action is urgently required, so that time acts as a lever to help participants stay focused on what is feasible and possible now. It is particularly useful when new relationships need to be forged between systems – organizations, communities, or whole sectors – to move things forward.

Like world café, OST is a method for opening up enquiry and less useful where a specific outcome is required. It is a good method for gathering information, generating ideas and forming new alliances; a broad consensus within the topics may emerge, particularly if there is a pressure for immediate action. If decision-making is needed, a longer timescale for the exercise is required.

Finally

This chapter has offered a rapid tour of some key elements of organizational theory and practice over recent decades, to illustrate the complexity of the context within which the group or team coach plies her/his trade, and to offer some conceptual tools for thinking about that context. Like skill in working with groups, systems-based coaching cannot be learned from a book but must be learned through experience. At the end of this book is a list of organizations that offer educational experiences along these lines.

Part 4

Team coaching

This chapter

More than half of all group coaching assignments are with intact teams.[102] In Chapter 5 we considered teams as 'nested systems', and described ways of thinking that allow us to engage with the complexity of team and larger-system interventions.

This chapter tackles team coaching from a different perspective, familiar to most team coaches: where the client is looking for specific outcomes with a specific team. In these circumstances, most team coaches design a pragmatic and goal-driven intervention to achieve the client's desired outcomes.

The wary coach does not, however, lose sight of the broader landscape. S/he pays attention to how the

This chapter contains:
- This chapter
- What is a team?
- The goals of team interventions
- Which of these goals are best met through team coaching?
- What is team coaching?
- Creating team coaching opportunities through other invitations
- Using team tools and models in coaching
- Common mistakes in using tools
- Seven rules to help us choose among tools for working with teams
- The contracting process: clarifying goals at the start
- Client relationship risks in team coaching
- Interviewing individual members of a team
- Working with the team's leader
- Dealing with unspoken expectations and dynamics
- When working with conflicting expectations
- Working with team difficulties: importance of timing
- Coaching virtual teams
- Finally

dynamics of the broader system are played out within the team, and in particular how the dynamics relate to any obstacles to the team achieving its outcomes. S/he is willing to raise these systemic issues with the team and the sponsor. This is in fact no different to the responsibility of the coach working with an individual, though team coaching requires a wider range of skills (see 'What are the characteristics of an effective group coach?' in Chapter 4). Chapters 2 to 5 illustrate the complexity of what might be happening in a particular team at any time, and underpin this more practically oriented chapter.

The chapter therefore opens by considering the goals of team coaching, and addresses the thoughtful practitioner about the essentials of the process. It discusses how to use tools (models or conceptual frameworks) with teams. It goes on to review some of the intricate issues and unspoken expectations arising in contracting and in managing client relationships, and discusses the timing of team interventions for maximum leverage. The discussion of team dynamics is continued in Chapter 10.

So much of the material in other chapters is relevant to teams that it is not all cross-referenced. In the box is a summary of the relevant major areas in other chapters.

Topic	Chapter
What is going on beneath the surface?	2, 3, 4
Systems theory of organizations	5
Difficult individuals and conflict	9
Difficult teams	10
Beginnings, middles and endings	11

What is a team?

Here is a typical definition of a team.

> A group of people who are interdependent with respect to information, resources and skills, and who seek to combine their efforts to achieve a common goal.[103]

Notice the similarities and differences with the systems view of teams described in 'Systems and teams' in Chapter 5. The idea of interdependence *within* the team is here, but little sense of how the team relates to the broader organization. The notion of goal or intention is also central, whereas in systems thinking it coexists in a complex web with how things *are*, as well as how the client would like them to be. This is what Argyris highlights in his contrast between 'theory-in-use' and 'espoused theory' (see the 'Mr Team' box later in this chapter). Most writing about teams concentrates on the latter too much, at the expense of the former.

The effective team coach always bears in mind that the team's explicit shared goal exists in a broader organizational context. A team also exists over time, so it usually has a history before the coaching intervention begins, with established communication patterns and a network of relationships. The coach reviews how functional these relationships are in achieving the goal(s).

The goals of team interventions

Team interventions are directed to the relationship between the team's goal and the team's capacity to carry it out. There are therefore three possible areas of focus.

1 *The team's goal.* For example: defining the goal, redefining it, breaking the goal into smaller steps, working out a strategy, planning implementation of part of the strategy, planning communication and negotiation of the strategy with other parts of the system, updating the strategy, assessing the longevity of the strategy, evaluating the success and/or impact of the strategy, refining or redefining the strategy . . .
2 *The team's capacity to collaborate to achieve the goal.* For example: listening to others' views carefully, sharing opinions frankly, enquiry and dialogue skills, asking the questions behind the questions, ability to tolerate uncertainty and not knowing the answer, learning to reflect together, ability to reorder priorities and work flexibly, ability to disagree constructively, building mutual trust, managing

interdependent tasks, influencing skills, mutual account-ability, giving and receiving feedback, overcoming bar-riers to communication, understanding each other, respect for others' viewpoints, ability to reach timely decisions together, commitment to and cooperation on decisions once made . . .

3 *The team members' skills in doing its work.* Skills that are necessary for individuals' work tasks; for example, using a new accounting package, interviewing, understanding colleagues from different cultural backgrounds, influ-encing skills, monitoring remotely, performance manage-ment, using the video-conferencing package . . .

The effective team coach always keeps in mind the possibility that the root of a team's incapacity lies elsewhere, in some other part of the broader system.

Which of these goals are best met through team coaching?

Team coaching is not the only kind of intervention teams seek to meet these goals, but for a high proportion of them, its framework offers the best prospect of success. This is due to four factors: the timeframe of the coaching relationship; its sensitivity in negotiating with clients; its attention to the individual; and the possibility of enhancing performance by improving communication skills.

A team exists over time as a 'nested system' connected to many intersecting systems, which means that it is constantly subject to changes small and large, affecting either what it should be doing, or how members work on it together. In this ever-shifting environment, rigid or simplistic models are not very useful.

Working on the goal

The development of business strategy is a subtle and complex process, which needs to be designed for constant refining and improvement as new information and new opportunities come to light. General Eisenhower commented that 'plans are nothing. Planning is everything.' It is the embedding of planning as a habitual and regular team process that is important. Team coaching is uniquely well suited to help senior teams embed the habits of planning, and design planning processes that are responsive to the particular industry. For middle management, the sharing of intelligence about implementation issues, and tackling problems together rather than reinventing the wheel, can offer the company significant design improvements and savings.

Working on team collaboration

In the area of team collaboration, team coaching has clear advantages over other methods, since it tackles communication issues directly and affords opportunity for practice. Careful thought and a light hand are needed to nurture a team's capacity for effective collaboration. In coaching, the team can work directly on its communication and interaction in real time, with a skilled coach to help it understand and overcome obstacles, and bring to light the 'undiscussables' (see 'Working with conflicting messages' in Chapter 10). It can agree goals for behaviour and processes, and can monitor these regularly through the coaching process. This can be particularly helpful when the team hits a stressful period. Under pressure good habits are easily lost, but coaching can help the team retain the gains it has made.

Team coaching assignments often have elements of both the first two foci – working together on the team's goal, and working on working towards it more effectively.

Skills development

The third group of interventions are simpler, on the face of it, and for some of them training is the right solution. Even with skills development, however, follow-up group coaching can offer a better efficacy rate if the skills are complex and interpersonal, and if it is critical that everyone acquire them to a good standard. Performance management is a good example of this. Group coaching following training can help people embed the skills, tackle problems, and share good practice, thus improving confidence and establishing a habit of reflecting together.

What is team coaching?

Team coaching is coaching a team to achieve a common goal, paying attention both to individual performance and to group collaboration and performance.

To be able to be coached, the team must be small enough (three to ten) for all the individuals to be actively involved when they are in one group (though you may still divide them into smaller groups at times). Working with a large team, a division or a whole small organization will require different methodology adapted to the needs of people in larger groups (discussed in Chapter 5). Team coaching, like all coaching, must also take place over time, and should involve some face time.

In team coaching, unlike learning group coaching, it is important that learning goals are shared. In most assignments a good deal of work is needed to arrive at this point, particularly if the client has done little preparation with team members. It is important for the coach to understand how individual goals might differ, and so, prudent to interview all members of a team individually before embarking on working with them together.

Creating team coaching opportunities through other invitations

Coaches are sometimes invited to help organizations with activities that are not team coaching, such as one-off team events.

A vast array of one-off activities are sold to companies as 'teambuilding', everything from rappelling up the north face of K2 to relaxing stress management days involving massage, visualization and herbal tea. The premise underlying them is that if the team shares a challenging or pleasant experience, it will always translate into stronger bonds when they get back to work. Sadly it is a premise for which there is little evidence, though there is nothing intrinsically wrong with giving staff a 'jolly' together or encouraging them to be kinder to each other. From our point of view as coaches, the problem is that as a result some clients have unrealistic expectations of what can be achieved in one event.

When invited to design and run one-off team events over one, two or three days, make enquiry into the client's goals. What outcomes do they hope for? While negotiating the contract, be scrupulous in limiting the agreed outcomes to what you know can be delivered within the time-frame. The 'away day' puts the question of transfer of learning – and the longevity of the good intentions expressed then – squarely in the frame. It is an unwary coach who promises lasting change to be delivered solely through this format. We are coaches precisely because we recognize that change is best supported through a relationship over time.

A one-off event can however be a useful kick-start to a coaching process, allowing the team to establish what problems it would like to solve, and its opening thoughts about what contributions its members can make. Negotiate for the event to be seen as the start of a process, and help the client define realistic intermediate outcomes for the event. If the focus is on the team's functioning or its communication, it is important to have individual conversations with the team members beforehand.

Contracting for shorter, non-coaching team interventions

- Be especially rigorous in clarifying and limiting the objectives so that you can deliver what you promise
- Inform the client clearly of the limits of what can be achieved
- If the goals of the intervention suggest that they might get better value from coaching, say so
- Make it clear that the event is a first step, and raise with the client the question of what further help might be needed.

If the outcomes are to do with improving the team's ability to communicate and work together, or to develop strategy in a complex environment, discuss with the client whether they wouldn't be better served by having a series of shorter sessions over time; in the first case so that they can then monitor and maintain any improvements, and in the second so that detailed analysis can be carried out between sessions and strategy refined in the light of new information.

Working with a senior team on larger events, such as whole-organization reviews or staff conferences, can also be an opportunity to help them think about how to embed the review/planning process, or desired changes. Structure the assignment as a mini-coaching process, with a review and debrief as well as preparation time. Chapter 5 describes some methods that can be used for this kind of event.

Using team tools and models in coaching

There are many, many books about teams: why some teams work, while others do not, has preoccupied writers for a hundred years. I do not seek to compete in this crowded market: this chapter is not about teams, but about *team coaching*. An understanding of teams as coaching groups helps the *reader* evaluate what might work best in various situations. In addition, this section includes advice about the uses of some long-established, well-known tools, likely to be familiar to most team coaches.

Thousands of conceptual models explain elements of team working, usually in terms of how an ideal team *should* work. There is a seemingly insatiable market for these 'team tools', and many seek, and not a few seek to create, the Holy Grail, the model of team working that will explain all complexities and prove the key to all difficulties.

I may as well begin by acknowledging my lack of belief in the Holy Grail. In twenty years of assisting teams to greater effectiveness and more robust communication, I have found value in many of the conceptual frameworks and tools that other practitioners have created, and have created not a few of my own. I have yet to find one that is good at all times and in all places.

In coaching teams, all tools require an artisan, or perhaps at times an artist. It is good to have a well-loaded toolbox, but this is not simply a process of attending as many seminars as possible on new approaches. Acquiring new tools can become a preoccupation at the expense of learning to wield the ones we already own with masterly skill, as all artisans must. In the end it is our judgement and our experience-honed instincts that lead us to pick up a particular instrument.

Common mistakes in using tools

The measure of a team coaching session is not how correctly we used a particular instrument, it is whether the team managed to talk to each other in a meaningful way about their work and how they work together. Did they reach any useful conclusions? Did they reach new insight or decide on courses of action to correct problems? If they did, you have earned your shilling. If they have thought about how to take their enquiry forward and maintain any improvements in collaboration, you have earned your bonus.

The bottom line is that in any team situation, there are several tools that may work. The search for the perfect tool is more often a sign of coach anxiety than anything else. Even when very experienced, it is perfectly normal to feel uncertain before a team coaching engagement. Every team is different, and no group entirely predictable, so we are entering the unknown, even if we do so with a lot of experience under our belt.

True preparation puts us in touch again with our own competence and confidence. For some, getting the performance anxiety over early by over-preparation beforehand is a means to calm. For others, it is a hiding to nothing. We must know, and trust, ourselves. In general, in an especially challenging situation it is better to use a tool we are familiar and confident with. Our own confidence in the team coaching process is of more value to the client team than a finely tuned but unfamiliar widget.

Another common mistake is to bombard the team with different tools or 'lenses' for viewing their situation, perhaps in the mistaken hope of giving them 'good value'. Closely allied to this is planning a packed agenda for the coaching session, particularly the first one. Don't. Conversations need time and you need to build this in. If there is no time to pursue the discussions they need to pursue, whatever is the point? If they seem unwilling to use the opportunities provided, you can pursue with them your own curiosities, such as, what isn't being said? Or, what led them to spend so much money and time in order *not* to talk?

Seven rules to help us choose among tools for working with teams

First, we need to keep in mind that all tools are simply a means of starting a conversation that the team need to have with each other. The conversations that teams hire a coach to facilitate are typically conversations that, for one reason or another, they are not keen on beginning. Reducing anxiety is therefore an important factor in tool selection. What tool uses language or concepts that are somewhat familiar to this particular team in this particular industry? Or if you want to shake up their thinking, what would be accessible enough that they will be provoked but not turned off? Whatever tool you choose, keep the objectives of the coaching firmly in mind.

Second, tools help mainly by giving a structure to the conversation that helps people feel safer at the beginning, to equalize the risk and the discomfort, to depersonalize any difficult feedback, and to give the team a sense of working together towards a goal. This is particularly important where the team is likely to be anxious, such as a collaboration-focused assignment with a team that is normally highly goal-focused. The more anxious the situation, the more highly structured and boundaried the coaching should be, and the more authoritative and containing the coach's demeanour. Manfred Kets de Vries has written an interesting article about the coach's role in a challenging, successful team feedback assignment,[104] which also demonstrates the importance of timing and leverage for change within the system.

Fourth, any model is ultimately a way of simplifying (over-simplifying, really) complex realities so that we can grasp them and talk about them. So choose a tool that is simple enough to be grasped and used by the team. Aim to understand the limitations as well as the strengths of the models you choose. Remember the pitfalls you have observed in using this particular tool before.

Related to this is the question of language. Simple language is best most of the time, and particularly where collaboration is the focus. Simple language speaks to the human in us as well as the professional. Language used in highly idiosyncratic ways can be off-putting to non-specialists. If you think the language used in a model may be a barrier, change it, or allow the group to change it, to something more usable.

Fifth, think about the likely effect of the tool on this team's situation. Are its concepts precise enough to open the necessary conversations? There are many tools that describe 'the ideal team' or identify the characteristics of dysfunctional teams. Is the tool general in its language – 'communication', 'trust', 'conflict' – which may simply lead the team to re-identify problems they already know they have, or does it provide routes into a more useful, specific discussion about what they want from, and are prepared to do for, each other?

Sixth, be eclectic in your sources, and scan sources that bring together many models, such as the books in the reading list by Gareth Morgan and Charles Handy. But look more widely than the management literature. Don't neglect conceptual models from other areas of life. For instance, I

Focus of the team coaching	Example of possible tool
Here's what I am like – what are you like? What does this mean for working together?	Myers-Briggs Type Indicator[105]
Feeling anxious or angry in our team	Tuckman model[106]
Change is a process including discomfort, not an announcement	Change curve[107]
Need to value skills of enquiry and dialogue (especially for a highly task-focused group)	Senge dialogue model[108]
Conflict and hostility	Drama triangle[109] (see also Chapter 10)
What skills do we each bring to the table? What skills are we strongest and weakest on? How do we fit together?	Belbin[110]
What style of relating do my individual reports/team members need?	Situational leadership[111]
Blaming culture or 'caring' organizations	Drama triangle
Planning change	Systems analysis tools such as fishbone diagram,[112] mind mapping[113]
Bringing a group together by focusing on shared purpose	SWOT (strengths, weaknesses, opportunities, threats) analysis[114]
Getting to grips with the realities of the business environment	PEST (political, environmental, social, technical) analysis[115]

use a model of influencing strategy that originally derives from the seventies peace movement. Have a magpie eye for what might be useful, and remember the power of the internet search engine in cross-checking tools.

Seventh, build your own library of favoured tools. Actually, this is a more non-conscious process than that sentence suggests. Certain tools and concepts come more readily to mind and hand than others, because you find them serviceable. Over time, the use and adaptation of favoured tools will give you an internal resource that sits alongside the planned use of a limited number of tools. When a new way of viewing something may be genuinely useful to the team you are working with, it will come to mind, arising from your mental index. Sit with it for a few minutes before introducing it, to assess whether it is truly helpful, or whether introducing it might relate more to your need to prove your usefulness.

Choosing tools for working with teams

- Remember the tool is a means to an end
- Choose and use a tool and a style in using it, to reduce anxiety
- Choose a tool that is fit for its purpose
- Don't overcomplicate things
- Be eclectic in looking for tools
- If *you* feel anxious, prefer a familiar and proven tool
- Stick to a small number of tools, don't bombard
- Don't identify yourself with the tool, just use it
- Notice and promote important team conversations that the tool provokes.

The contracting process: clarifying goals at the start

The goals of team coaching must be sufficiently precise that a view can be taken about whether or not they have been reached. 'Improving communication' is a field of activity, not a coaching goal. What communications are difficult? How would improvement be recognized? Imprecise goals deny the coach a sense of achievement, since their accomplishment cannot be tested.

Contracting is not simply a matter of the coaching sponsor arriving at a form of words about *their* goal with which the coach is comfortable. To be successful, the goals of team coaching must be owned by the team members, requiring a process of negotiation with the team. How much of this negotiation remains to be done as the coaching begins varies greatly, depending on the quality of the preparation, by both client and coach. The absolute minimum at the outset of coaching is a re-examination of the 'draft' goals and a checking out of agreement, or at least consent.

One useful way of checking how far consent and understanding reach is to ask team members to give intermediate steps that would indicate movement towards the goals, or to ask about the contribution of the coaching to achieving the goals. This last can be a starting point in the group refining its goals and defining the ground rules it wishes to establish for the coaching.

Contracting is therefore a critical part of the team coaching process, and acts as a benchmark for all further interactions between coach and team. The contract is more than the written statement about the assignment, important touchstone though that is. In Chapter 8 there is a checklist for contracting in group supervision, which could also be used as a basis for a team coaching contract, ignoring the headings that do not apply.

Contracting is a subtle process, and cannot be reduced to words on a page. During the process the team coach may sense that more is being asked than the words suggest. It is important to pursue these feelings and encourage the client or sponsor to make explicit their unspoken hopes, so that they can be discussed and their feasibility assessed. See also below 'Dealing with unspoken expectations and dynamics'.

Vignette: Contracting for a change programme

Ali is approached by Janet, VP of the UK division of a service-based company with whom she has worked before. Janet wants Ali to work with middle managers on a change programme to introduce tighter performance management. The middle managers are cynical because they feel that the 'top' has a different view every month of what will help the business. This time Janet knows it's different – the new global performance management standards will ultimately see these managers out of a job if they don't comply.

The contract is to coach the middle managers individually at first, and then to bring them together as a group to work on managing the change. Ali is not sure at what point to do this, though timing seems to be under her control; she has a budget and *carte blanche* about how to carry out the coaching assignment.

Janet also has to develop implementation systems for the new standards – an area in which Ali is expert. Janet is keen to seek her advice.

As Ali struggles to shape the contract from initial meetings with Janet and her managers, she realizes that Janet has not laid out what specific changes she wishes to see.

Issues

There is a difference of view about facts. Janet and Ali know that financial conditions compel the company to be serious about change this time, but the managers have not taken this reality on board.

There is no clarity about the indicators if the change were successfully implemented; the sponsor hasn't refined her objectives much beyond 'they have to change'. It is therefore impossible to define clear outcomes for the coaching. Nor have the individual performance issues been articulated clearly.

There is flattery in the invitation to the coach: in the approach, in the '*carte blanche*', in the invitation to consult on implementation systems. This could seduce Ali into being less rigorous than usual.

Analysis

A greater degree of clarity about objectives is essential.

A commonly understood set of business facts is essential. This is Janet's responsibility.

The invitation to consult is flattering, but it is a different role from coaching. How would it impact on the coaching assignment? The impact isn't necessarily negative – maybe the room for manoeuvre on implementation represents an opportunity to involve the managers in design. Ali would have to remain clear which role she was occupying at each point in the process.

Next steps

Ali meets Janet again to refine the objectives of the change programme and the coaching. They agree it is essential for the group of managers to get to grips with the new reality in the company, and that this is best done in a group. Ali coaches Janet to handle the meeting and accompanies her.

At the meeting, Janet spells out the company's change of policy and the economic conditions that drive it; by the end of an uncomfortable meeting, most of the managers have 'got it'. Ali convenes a follow-up meeting a week later to help the managers work on *their* objectives. This leads to agreement on a series of meetings to manage the change and some clarification between the goals of the team coaching and the individual coaching.

Janet discusses individual targets with each manager, and then each has a three-way meeting with Janet and Ali, to discuss these in line with the programme.

Comments

Since the challenge of this new situation is shared, primarily group-based coaching is likely to be most effective, augmented by individual coaching as needed. Tackling the challenge as a group, including acknowledging cynical as well as positive feelings, will result in a team that has common understandings and shared tasks – as fellow-sufferers at worst, and as partners when more positive feelings can be galvanized.

Ali's first achievements are the clarification of goals and the managers' realization of the inevitability of the change. Once this idea is viewed 'in the most serviceable light – first as a settled, and second, as a good'[116] thing, Ali uses every opportunity to engage the managers in thinking about how to implement. Some of the questions she asks are:

- How could you gain from the change?
- How could the service improve from the change?
- How could staff gain from the change?
- What do you value about the service as it is?
- How could that be preserved in the change?
- How could it be strengthened?

The quality of the prior relationship means that Ali starts the assignment with a good deal of trust 'in the bank'. This enables her to get further, faster than she might have at the start of a new coaching relationship.

The box below sets out possible stages in a team coaching assignment.

Team coaching checklist

The initial contact – who made it? What was the route to you?

Contracting – discussing goals with sponsor, team leader and team, and agreeing broad goals

Individual interviews to explore issues in more depth

↓

Presenting the findings to the sponsor, team leader and team, and discussing to refine goals and outcomes

↓

Agreeing outcome and processes, group and individual

↓

Beginning the coaching process

↓

Reviewing the coaching process

↓

Refining and recontracting, or completing the coaching process

Client relationship risks in team coaching

In team coaching there are always at least two clients. There is the sponsor – the budget-holder who commissions the work, often the team leader – and there is the team with whom you will be working. If the sponsor is not the same person as the leader of the team in question, you have three clients, each potentially with their own ideas about what is needed. And one of them consists of several people. The coach must have the tact to make it clear to the sponsor and the team leader that success in the coaching relies on the team having ownership of its goals, which requires a measure of flexibility and negotiation in determining them. This is the first step the coach takes onto the tightrope of balancing the needs of several stakeholders.

Where the person commissioning the coaching is not the most senior member of the team, it is prudent to meet that senior colleague before the coaching commences, to ensure that they are in agreement with the goals, and support coaching as a method.

There is always a risk in team coaching of being caught between competing or conflicting objectives. When such conflicts develop, the coach should minimize the risk by being honest with all parties, and referring back to them the question of the true goals of the coaching assignment. You may often have to help them negotiate these with each other. See 'Dealing with unspoken expectations and dynamics' in this chapter, and 'Working with unconscious and unspoken conflicts' and 'Working with conflicting messages' in Chapter 10. You have to be rigorous too, in differentiating their desired outcomes from the contribution that the coaching will make towards achieving them.

Where the focus of the coaching is strategic, it may be adequate to meet the team together to prepare for the work, or to build an initial preparation period into the coaching. For any assignment where improvements in communication are desired, it is wise to speak to the team members individually before embarking on facilitating an exchange of views. In longer assignments, when it is time to review the work, it can be useful to re-interview individuals to see how far perspectives have changed.

Interviewing individual members of a team

Interviewing individual members of a team prior to a team coaching assignment is invaluable where any of the goals of the coaching are in the second area of collaborative skills, or where the team has been 'stuck' for some time. It will help you not only to discover how each person sees the coaching and what goals they have for it, but to uncover the unspoken conflicts or other hidden obstacles to better collaboration and performance. There are two purposes to these meetings: to inform yourself, and to prepare the team members; like any two-way conversation, both parties can gain.

The interviews can reinforce the goals of the group coaching and prepare each person to engage as fully as possible. For example, if to disagree constructively is a goal of the team coaching, interviews will allow you to explore in advance with each member their habitual responses, and the desired ones. For example, some people equate disagreement with aggression, and are scared of it (for more on this issue, see 'Dealing with anger in a group' in Chapter 9).

Set up these individual interviews explicitly and carefully with each person as having the overall goal of assisting the team's communication to be more forthright and respectful. Commit only to a degree of confidentiality consistent with that goal. Always have in mind how what you hear will affect the team sessions.

A sweeping commitment to total confidentiality is a hostage to fortune. If someone tells you a troubling or toxic secret, take up with them immediately the question of how to handle it in the group. Would they be willing to raise it? What would help them do so? Would they be willing for you to raise it? What about first informing the team leader (if s/he is not an actor in the story) or raising it with her/him (if s/he is)?

If a team member tells you something important that s/he is not willing to have discussed in the group, consider why. There are sometimes good personal reasons for keeping a secret, but secrets are rarely good for teams. Why has the team member told you if they do not wish the matter aired? So you will feel sympathy, or let them off the hook? To sabotage the process? Because the secret is too troubling to keep? Who else knows this secret? Find out, and consider with the team member the impact, on herself/himself and others, of continuing to keep the secret.

Working with the team's leader

Team coaches have to preserve a dual loyalty to the team and to its leader. If the coach cannot form an effective working alliance with the most powerful member of the team, and command the respect and trust of both team and leader, the long-term impact of the assignment will always be in question. In order to maintain the alliance and manage this tension, it is wise to arrange individual sessions with the team leader alongside the group sessions. At times there will be tensions because the roles, and therefore the needs, of team and leader are different.

Systems thinking helps us understand this. The leader's role is the most exposed and the loneliest in the team. S/he typically represents the team/subsystem upwards and outwards in critical negotiations with other subsystems. S/he is most responsible for feedback from and to other systems. Constantly at the boundary of the team subsystem, the leader is more subject to the pressures for the team to change; at times this may create a distance with other team members. Further, the leader's role requires her/him to address performance shortfalls with individuals. Finally, in working upwards with other systems or subsystems, the leader has less direct power, and must rely more heavily on influencing skills. S/he cannot always 'succeed'.

These problems are exacerbated in senior teams, where it can be difficult to bring everyone together, and all too easy to focus on managing downwards to avoid facing harder realities together. If the team leader is also the CEO of the organization, the issues of isolation and risk are redoubled. There may be no one but the coach with whom the CEO can be completely honest and so find a neutral reflective space.

The effective team coach forges an alliance with the team's leader so that they are partners in the work, and at the same time retains the trust of team members. At times s/he will need to help leader and team bridge a gap, or provide private feedback to the leader on how s/he is relating to the rest of the team. This 'live' in-team coaching offers leaders a unique opportunity to extend their leadership skills. For all these reasons regular sessions with the team leader are needed in any team coaching assignment. If the team leader is also the client commissioning the work, you need clear lines of communication with her/him in that distinct role, which may be best approached in separate meetings. If the sponsor is a different individual, the coach's reporting arrangement there should also be transparent.

In order to preserve transparency and trust, the coach must make it clear to the team that s/he is also meeting the leader individually, and encourage them to air their feelings and ideas about this. In a tense team, prompting may be

Vignette: Preparing for lean times

The CEO of a not-for-profit organization housing people with disabilities was gifted, and cursed, with foresight. His company had expanded rapidly by securing funding to develop innovative new services, and it had an enviable reputation for high quality, far beyond the minima set in contract specifications. While still expanding, and long before his not-for-profit competitors, he understood not only that the period of growth was ending, but that in future the survival of services and the companies themselves would be under severe threat. New Government tendering criteria favoured competition from private companies relatively unfettered by concern for service standards, and so able to undercut costs.

For the CEO and subsequently for his senior managers, this was agonizing. Not-for-profit executives characteristically feel passionate commitment to the company's goals, and here the 'double bottom line' of meeting the goals while balancing the books seemed impossible in the new circumstances. How could the funding now available secure the excellent services they had always striven to deliver?

During a long-term monthly coaching assignment, the coach assisted the CEO in clarifying the implications of his insight. In his sessions and the team coaching sessions alike, an important task was coming to terms with the new realities. The time lag between this happening for the CEO and the rest of his team was a tension addressed in the team sessions, as were their own fears about the future, painful feelings about the cuts they had to make to reduce costs, and about the anger directed towards them by the staff. At times tensions between them ran high, but by the end of the assignment they had reduced costs by 20% while refining service specifications to protect essential components, equipping themselves to compete in the new tendering environment.

necessary, though many people will understand why the difference in the leader's role makes it essential. Ask the team members to consider and name what the benefits and risks to them might be.

Dealing with unspoken expectations and dynamics

All coaching is about helping the team gain or achieve something: something they do not have or cannot manage at present. Even where the coaching is to make a good performance excellent, the aim is to reach or recover a desired

---

Vignette: Stuck

Carolyn had been working with the top team of a financial services company for nine months. The focus was developing a five-year strategic plan. At first they had responded well, but as time went on several of the team failed to do agreed work and gradually the process was grinding to a halt. Carolyn felt less and less interested in the project, and had to force herself to make contact.

In supervision it became clear that under her boredom lay frustration and anger. She had tried many tactics to get the team moving again, and nothing had worked. She did not know what to do next, felt anxious, and had a strong impulse to 'sack' the client.

The supervision group explored how Carolyn's stuckness and anger mirrored the team's. The assignment had left her with indigestible feelings of anxiety and futility. Feeling somewhat relieved, Carolyn concluded that she should carefully monitor her feelings at the next session, and use them to shape questions to the team about the gap between what they said and what they did. She prepared a few questions in advance: How it happened that no progress was made despite everyone's apparent wish that it should? What frustrated them in the work? What worried them about the future? What did the team gain from the absence of a plan? What else was more important than the plan?

standard of work. The contract represents coach's and client's best and latest understanding about desired team outcomes.

Any experienced team coach has at times had a non-rational sense of more being expected than they had signed up for, a reality gap between explicit, acknowledged coaching goals and the felt, unspoken experience of being asked for something different. (Chapter 2 explains how this kind of unconscious expectation is communicated.)

It is critical that the coach gain some understanding of these unspoken expectations or 'felt realities'; the risk of ignoring them is to proceed with work that fits the written contract, but is experienced by the team as irrelevant. The risk of trying to meet the expectations without acknowledging them is worse, since it usually means trying to meet conflicting expectations, and therefore setting oneself up to fail.

We may be caught in unconscious team or organizational conflicts when:

- the felt expectations do not match what is written in the contract
- there is an unspoken sense that the coaching is 'beside the point'
- there is a sense of dissatisfaction with the coaching
- agreed actions are consistently not acted upon
- the feeling doesn't match what is said
- we feel discomfort or dissatisfaction we cannot quite put our finger on
- there is a sense of being invited to play a part for which we have not auditioned.

There are many, many possible unconscious communications in team coaching work. It is an area where skilled and psychologically informed supervision is invaluable to all coaches, however experienced. Understanding and working with the unconscious dynamics of organizations is not an area for self-help or 'going it alone'. Further, many coaches do not want to specialize in working in depth with these dynamics, they simply want help to deal with specific obstacles in their team coaching assignments. Here too supervision can help.

Some books devoted to these issues, and some educational opportunities, are suggested in Part 6. While training to specialize on group dynamics is lengthy, expensive and personally demanding, there are shorter workshops and programmes designed to extend the understanding of non-specialists.

For most coaches, using supervision to recognize when this kind of situation has arisen, and to consider the most promising courses of action, is the most practicable course. Group supervision is especially helpful for coaches working with teams, because the complex dynamics of the team situation can be mirrored and worked with live in the supervision group.

When working with conflicting expectations

If we sense that all is not as it seems, a practical first step is to check out whether what we are feeling mirrors some feeling in the team or organization. Look for clues in what is said that might indicate this, and follow them up. Are they expecting from you what others expect of them? Are they communicating some feelings about the work or the state of their industry? Ask team members what is not being said, what they are holding back on, or what the unwritten rules are. By pursuing these questions, at the very least you will gain some material that can be considered in supervision.

In the following box are some questions to help the team coach begin to clarify the nature of this kind of gap.

> ### Understanding unspoken expectations
>
> * Is there any conflict between the expectations of the team and the expectations of the budget-holder commissioning the work?
> * Who/what am I invited to be at a feeling level? (Give your imagination free rein – left-of-field non-rational intuition is your friend)
> * Is there any parallel in this organization to the experience I am having? (For example, does it reflect what customers/service users expect, or mirror a threat in the organization or its environment?)

Chris Argyris describes the difference between conscious and unconscious expectations as a conflict between 'espoused theory' (what I say) and 'theory-in-use' (deduced from actions). Here is an example[117] (see also 'Argyris' theory of organizational defences' in Chapter 10).

Mr Team

Espoused theory	Theory-in-use
We must learn to work as a team. The era of the loner has gone.	I will decide by myself to reject the ideas I do not like, even if everyone else wishes to discuss them.
We are all in control of the family jewels.	I will be in control, and you will give up the control whenever the discussion is not to my liking.
We must learn not to hold back and hedge when in a crunch.	I can hold back and hedge when in a crunch.

The culture has taught individuals not to be effective team members.	When my cabinet acts as an effective team in designing a workshop on team building with which I disagree, I will act as an individual and ignore the team.
Maybe executives like myself have been too soft on our subordinates.	I will be soft on myself and deny that this is what I am doing.
We must examine all the factors that inhibit the building of the team.	I will not permit discussion of my fancy footwork.

Once through reflection and supervision we have arrived at some working hypotheses about the conflicting communications, we can consider our next steps. In coaching teams, we need to bring some of the 'felt reality' into the light of day, since it is the unrecognized conflicts that frustrate change. The specifics of how much, and how it should be framed, must be thought about on a case-by-case basis. There is further material about unconscious team dynamics in Chapter 10.

Working with team difficulties: importance of timing

In working with teams, you do not begin with a clean page. Relationship and communication patterns, including damaging ones, are already established in teams before coaching begins, except in new teams. Members do not have equal power; and the distribution of power only matches the organizational chart to some degree.

'Family' is a useful analogy in understanding how teams differ from other kinds of group. Human individuals begin their learning in a group, usually that of their birth family. Some families are better than others at enabling learning, and all families have their strengths and weaknesses in this regard. Similarly in a team, a more or less functional compromise for learning has been arrived at between the various needs and predilections of the team's members, particularly of the senior or most influential members.

Hence for a team to learn and change, some existing processes usually need to be dismantled and put together in a more functional way – which will involve discomfort, at the least. The 'undiscussables' must be discussed (see 'Working with conflicting messages' in Chapter 10). It is in this process of clarifying communication and interpersonal learning to help the team achieve its goals, that group coaching can make its uniquely powerful contribution.

Systems thinking shows us that the felt need for team coaching will be balanced by resistance to change, within both the team and the wider organization. Failure to recognize and work with this is why so many short-term team interventions fail to make a lasting difference.

At challenging times, however, there are significant risks and equally great potential rewards from team coaching. In response to stress, complexity and differentiation are lost, and anxiety and ineffectiveness can predominate. On the other hand, to survive, the system has, in any event, to change. A skilful team coaching intervention at this point can harness the forces for change, and team members can seize the moment to learn a more adaptive way of functioning together.

Timing is therefore critical in team coaching; it is of most value when the system is undergoing change. Even the most challenging business circumstances create a promising opportunity for real change, if handled capably; other pressures provide leverage making a positive outcome from team coaching more likely.

Coaching virtual teams

In many corporations teams now exist that do not routinely meet face to face at all, working through email, data transfer, live messaging, telephone conferencing, video-conferencing and other distance technologies. In circumstances where there is no possibility of a team meeting face to face, as with global multinational teams, team coaching is probably best approached through the team's normal communication methods, and in particular through video-conferencing, which offers participants more information and relational possibilities than telephone or written communications.

Technological advances in video-conferencing seem likely to lead to its far greater use over the next decades. It will be interesting to learn, as video-conferencing sophistication increases, how that measures up to being physically together in the same room. A common use is among multinational teams, which raises a further set of questions. Although video-conferencing gives access to more non-conscious information than the telephone, the ability to interpret it across cultures may not be well developed, whether in the same room or on different continents and a variety of time zones. Global teams have become a reality through advances in communication technology, but will a comparable investment be made in developing the human parts of the interaction?

Some research suggests that virtual teams experience common workplace relationship problems at much higher rates of frequency than normal.[118] Without attention to a broader and more conscious education in interpreting non-conscious communications, including the differences between cultures, technology may deliver only the illusion of communication, with greater ease in avoiding the discomfort (felt in the room) that can push us to learn about each other.

Experience suggests that web- and telephone-based groups work more effectively if they have also met in person. The coach to a virtual team should insist on the necessity of at least one face-to-face encounter, to build a sense of common purpose and mutual relationship, and to begin to tackle communication barriers rooted in cross-cultural misunderstanding. If the client cannot agree to this, be as precise as possible about the limitations this places on the coaching outcomes. See also 'Group telephone coaching' in Chapter 7.

When working with teams:

- be rigorous in clarifying their goals
- test what is happening against goals
- have attention to how the power relations affect the coaching
- form a working alliance with the team's leader
- practise transparency in your interactions with leader and team
- pay attention to anything contradicting explicit goals, and bring it into the light of day
- pay attention to shared values and assumptions
- be willing to ask the 'stupid' question
- be willing to ask the discomforting question.

Finally

The next chapter turns to learning groups. There is more material about teams in Chapter 10.

Learning group coaching

This chapter

In the last chapter we focused on teams. Most people have an idea what a team is, but what are learning groups, and what are their uses in organizations?

Learning groups are specially convened to work on learning tasks, focusing on the needs of the individual members rather than the group as a whole. In this chapter we consider four variants and their contribution to individual learning:

- action learning
- Balint groups
- group telephone coaching
- coaching sessions within training and management development programmes.

This chapter contains:
- This chapter
- Learning group coaching versus team coaching
- What is action learning?
- The origins and development of action learning
- What happens in an action learning set?
- What is the structure of an action learning set?
- Setting up action learning protocols
- What is action learning used for?
- Balint groups
- Group telephone coaching
- Coaching sessions within management development programmes and other ongoing training groups
- Finally on learning groups: users' views of the interpersonal skill gains

Although supervision groups are also learning groups, they are not discussed here, as the next chapter is devoted to them.

Learning group coaching versus team coaching

Learning groups are groups brought together specifically for the purposes of learning, and their members are not part of the same intact team. Their functioning follows the same basic group laws set out in Chapters 2, 3 and 4.

One key difference for the coach practitioner lies in the goals. Whereas team coaching has shared goals relating to team performance, learning group members each have individual goals, and this diversity is itself central to the richness of the learning experience. The purpose of a learning group is the individual learning of its members.

When coaching a team, the coach starts with a good deal of learning to do about 'how things are done around here'. When beginning work with a learning group of relative strangers, such as an action learning set, these constraints are less powerful, particularly if the members are from different organizations. The members' 'how things are done around here' beliefs differ from each other, giving new points of comparison and learning.

There are different challenges at the start of a learning group: a group of strangers may initially be wary of each other, and will be evaluating the skill and authority of the coach. On the other hand, it is easier for the coach to influence the culture of the group, since no previous culture exists, and because at first s/he will tend to be seen as the leader. Further, a group of people who are not immediate colleagues have relatively few hidden agendas, because their *only* major working relationship is in starting together as fellow and mutual learners.

The group coach therefore has far more influence in setting the tone of the group as a positive learning environment. The successful group coach melds her/his new learning group into a 'project team with the purpose of learning', and working relationships can develop that are at once profoundly supportive and profoundly challenging. We are going to examine four types of learning group: the first is action learning.

What is action learning?

Although there is a common-knowledge idea that we learn from experience, a brief survey of human history confirms that we do not always learn, and that there is no guarantee that lessons learned by one generation will be remembered by the next. All coaches know that people vary greatly in how well they use the lessons of their experience.

Action learning is a means of structuring an individual's learning from experience, using the resources of other individuals in a group, to enable fuller, more effective learning. It is a rigorous method with benefits in:

- seeing the bigger picture
- understanding complex situations more fully
- reviewing and exploring options for action.

Action learning is valuable in learning to deal with situations where there is no clear 'right answer' and the individual must choose between several possible courses of action. The action learning process results in a broader range of options being thoroughly explored; chosen strategies are then put into action, revisited and evaluated over time, in order to be refined and progressed.

Action learning groups are traditionally called 'sets'.

The origins and development of action learning

Action learning is perhaps the mostly widely known form of learning group coaching in the UK, with a sufficiently long history to produce research and a literature.[119] Elements of the approach are routinely incorporated into leadership development programmes and postgraduate study. Action learning was invented in the middle of the last century by Reg Revans, a scientist, athlete and iconoclastic management educator who concluded that most management education was ineffective. Here is Revans' own definition of action learning:

Learning ... is ... the more appropriate use, by reinterpretation, of the subject's existing knowledge, including his recollection of past lived experiences. This reinterpretation is a social process carried on among two or more learners, who, by the apparent incongruity of their exchanges, frequently cause each other to examine afresh many ideas that they would otherwise have continued to take for granted, however false or misconceived.

(Revans 1982, p. 627)

Revans was frustrated by the lack of applicability of what management schools taught, and wanted to enable managers to apply their learning to work problems they had personal responsibility for resolving, and on which they would have to take action. For Revans, the two key elements of learning were questioning, which can produce insight, and 'programmed' or theoretical knowledge. Combined, the two can produce learning, as expressed in Revans' formula $P + Q = L$.

Action learning ideas have great flexibility, and over time practitioners have used, interpreted and modified Revans in a variety of ways. As a result there are significant variations in methodology, but research suggests that 75% of UK practitioners agreed on some core elements:[120]

- sets of about six people
- action on real tasks or problems at work, with learning from reflection on actions taken
- tasks/problems are individual rather than collective and chosen by individuals
- questioning as the main way to help participants proceed with their tasks/problems
- group coaches are used.

In itself this unanimity is a tribute to the robustness of the method; I would add these further elements to round out a picture of action learning:

- a contract to meet regularly for mutual aid in learning
- turn-taking so focus is shared between group members
- a fundamentally open approach to the 'problem'
- a reflective stance expressed in a pace that allows 'time to think'.

What happens in an action learning set?

A group of about six meet regularly with a coach, usually for a day a month. Some groups are time-limited, for example to a six- or twelve-month period; some are open-ended or tied to the completion of a programme. The group members are normally relative strangers to each other, not rivals or close colleagues.

Action learning introduces regular reflection into the work process, with the focus on individuals' current needs and concerns rather than having a fixed content (as in traditional training courses). At the outset, each member chooses a learning objective on which s/he will work in the set. Learning objectives *must* relate to real work for which the member is currently responsible, though the focus may be as broadly strategic, or as tightly focused on managing particular people, projects or issues, as the individual wishes.

At each meeting, each member of the set has a turn in which to report back on the action they have taken since the previous meeting, to reflect on successes and failures, and to plan their next steps in taking things forward. During the turn, the rest of the group must assist the turn-taker *only* through *listening* and *questioning*. Each member must use their own reactions to what they hear to frame open questions to help the turn-taker understand their situation more fully.

This is a demanding and rigorous process that both makes the experience of the whole group available to each member *and* requires each member to think carefully about how best to frame a question for the person to whom it is addressed; thus interpersonal skills are developed as a by-product of the process, even in people who have good levels of skill at the start. Another side-benefit is in the development of questioning or enquiry skills, of great value in understanding complex problems in any modern business context.

The multiple perspectives of all the group members enrich the reflection process so that many more perspectives, and therefore options, are considered than is possible in individual coaching, and in a more rigorous and thought-provoking way than ordinary group discussion. Further, each member of the group gains profound insight into the challenges of other members, broadening their understanding of the leadership role.

What is the structure of an action learning set?

Despite the unanimity of practitioners about the core elements, there is no standardized structure for action learning. The one described here is my own practitioner version, developed through more than fifteen years of practice and enriched by an emphasis on the group interaction element and its value for learning. It is in line with the core elements described above.

The timings require about one hour per member, so a group of six takes a full day, adding some time for breaks; timings can be adjusted slightly where time is more limited, but the easy pace of action learning is an important feature, so they cannot, for example, be halved. The total time allocated in this turn is 55 minutes, which gives the group coach five minutes' leeway per hour, making it possible to keep the group to time, allow for comfort breaks, etc.

Structure of an action learning 'turn': guide for the group coach	
5 minutes	**Presenter outlines the issue**, problem or topic as they see it.
30 minutes	**Exploration of the issue.** Listening and questioning. Pace gentle enough to allow space for thought, 'open' questions that can offer the presenter a different perspective.
5 minutes	**Summing up.** Encourage the presenter to take a lead here in saying what the most useful lines of questioning have been, what their thinking is now, whether there have been any shifts in

how they see the issue. Discourage major new questions (though you may have to live with one or two at the start of this section).

15 minutes   **Review the turn together: 'thoughts unuttered, feelings unexpressed'.**
- What were the 'thoughts unuttered, feelings unexpressed'?
- What were the things you were bursting to say but couldn't translate to a question?
- Did you feel a strong urge to give advice (and how well did you resist)?
- What feelings did you experience?
- How does the presenter think those feelings might relate to the situation?
- How did you feel using the action learning protocols?
- How could you improve in using the action learning protocols?
- Resist problem-solving during this section – it is a debrief for everyone, though it may help further the presenter's understanding.

The 'thoughts unuttered, feelings unexpressed' review of each turn allows not only for debriefing but also for a freer exchange, which usually augments the learning about the topic and always develops members' sensitivity to their interpersonal interactions. Over time, knowing that this review is coming makes it easier for set members to conform to the rigour of the listening and questioning section.

Setting up action learning protocols

At the outset every action learning set needs to acclimatize itself to the discipline of interacting only through listening and questioning within the turns. Here is an example of the kind of advice the group coach may offer new set members at the outset.

When listening and questioning

Do:

- listen carefully for content and meaning
- put up with uncertainty
- ask open questions.

Don't:

- ask too many questions – make a couple of good ones really count
- ask lots of questions to understand every detail of the situation. It doesn't matter if you don't, you are not being asked for an 'expert opinion'!
- ask questions that are thinly veiled advice, such as 'had you thought of . . .?'
- create 'rush', such as by asking a question when the turn-taker hasn't had a chance to think about the previous one.

Similarly every set needs to develop its own version of the protocols or ground rules, which builds on the core elements outlined above. This is best done as a collaboration between coach and members. Here is a typical set of ground rules generated in that way.

> **Action learning protocols**
>
> - Mutual respect
> - Problems without right answers
> - Learning from experience
> - Action-related
> - Listening and questioning
> - Process as important as content
> - Thinking and feeling are equally important
> - Turn-taker in charge of own learning
> - Easy pace.

What is action learning used for?

Action learning was originally developed as a means of enabling powerful individual learning through a highly structured group process. Its focus is on making use of all available information and insight in tackling complex problems, developing thinking and the practical application of insight. It provides a reference group that helps maintain motivation for taking action over time.

Action learning allows executives the regular opportunity to reflect, and through questioning, speculation, deduction and exploration within the group, to arrive at new working hypotheses about achieving goals. New ideas are tested against reality, and plans refined in the light of trials and further experience. Rather than a 'quick fix', learning becomes a continuous experience, more fruitful and more profound. Versions of action learning are used in many leadership and management development programmes.

A significant body of anecdotal evidence and a growing body of research[121] suggests that action learning has many unanticipated benefits, such as the refining of skills in the participating individuals. Research into how group membership develops confidence and competence underpins the themes of Chapter 4.[122]

Skills gains from action learning

- Interpersonal sensitivity and skill
- Reflective capacity and the development of habits of reflecting with others
- Skills of enquiry that allow more data to be used in problem-solving
- Improved meeting skills through greater use of enquiry[123]
- Greater capacity to deal with uncertainty and change
- Over time, the development of greater flexibility through internalizing multiple viewpoints.

Action learning is a flexible technique and can be adapted to many different circumstances. This is not without risk, since departure from the core elements will dilute the method and rob it of some of its power. Nevertheless it can be used in many ways, for example by project teams and intact teams to progress collective goals; in coaching sessions within longer training programmes to allow participants to reflect on how to apply what they have learned. In larger organizations, action learning is used cross-departmentally as a vehicle for culture change or to implement a change in management strategy.

Action learning is primarily an investment in individuals, and its value to individuals who have experienced it is not in much doubt. For organizations seeking change through investment in key individuals this is not problematic. Measuring outcomes at an organizational level is, however, not straightforward, since it leads us to the long-vexed question of how far individual learning becomes organizational learning.[124]

Balint groups

Like action learning, Balint groups are a structured way of reflecting with others in a group. They are named after their originators, psychoanalysts Enid and Michael Balint. Balint groups were originally developed in the 1950s as a means of educating doctors in managing the doctor–patient relationship, emphasizing the importance of emotional and personal understanding and aiming at a more successful therapeutic alliance between doctor and patient. Today they are still most widely used within Health Services across the world. They deserve a wider audience because, like action learning, they offer a simple methodology for reflecting in groups, provided that the protocols are rigorously followed.

Balint group protocols

- Respectful behaviour, presenter owns her/his own learning
- Problems without right answers
- Practising detachment, silence, listening and waiting
- Learning from each other's perspectives
- Thinking and feeling are equally important
- Easy pace.

As in action learning, Balint groups use a turn-taking methodology, with a focus on one particular member presenting their learning issue at any given moment, for assistance from the group. Unlike action learning sets, not every member presents their work at each meeting; instead there is a rolling programme that spreads the turns evenly over time.

Unlike action learning, there is relatively little interaction between the presenter (or problem-owner) and the rest of the group about the issue or problem under discussion.

Structure of a 'turn' in a Balint group

10 minutes	**Presenter outlines the issue,** problem or topic as s/he sees it. Reflection group listens.
20–25 minutes	**Reflection group explores the issue as though it were their own issue. Presenter sits 'outside' the group and observes the others exploring the issue.** The aim of the reflection group is to understand the issue as fully as possible and to explore their own associations to it. There is no requirement to 'solve' the problem or 'resolve' the issue.
5–10 minutes	**Presenter sums up.** The presenter comes back 'into' the group and presents her/his thinking about the issue following the discussion, commenting if s/he wishes on parts of the discussion that forwarded her/his thinking. Reflection group listens carefully without comment. The presenter does not need to evaluate every aspect of the discussion – s/he need only pick up on what has furthered her/his own thinking.
15 minutes	**Review the experience together.** Was there a strong urge? What feelings did you experience? Did the presenter, or someone else in the story, appear to have similar feelings? How might those feelings relate to the situation? How did you find using the Balint protocols? How could you improve in using the protocols? Resist further discussion – this section is a debrief for everyone, even though it may also further the presenter's understanding.

Instead the presenter and the rest of the group take it in turns to speak, requiring careful listening. Like action learning, the coach must ensure that the review does not become a discussion extending the turn.

It is interesting to look at Balint groups alongside action learning sets. Both are methods of reflective practice, but the Balint method is simpler and less interactive, particularly in a classic form that doesn't include the review of each turn. Its origins in the medical profession suggest that it might have value for those whose work allows very little time for reflection; it enforces silent reflection on the problem-owner, and careful listening on the group as a whole. These factors alone give it value for time-poor professions and professionals.

Group telephone coaching

Telephone and even email/live messaging coaching is on the increase, reflecting the growing pressure on time and staff development budgets in working life. In team coaching it can be a helpful adjunct to face-to-face meetings, and for some global teams, the most readily accessible way of communicating live. See also 'Coaching virtual teams' in Chapter 6

Time-poor modern executives can find it easier to slot in a telephone than a face-to-face session, and so individual telephone coaching is growing. Also, many companies impose travel restrictions during lean times. Telephone coaching is not equivalent to face-to-face, but has value, especially where the face-to-face version is not available. In one-to-one coaching where coach and client have established a good alliance face-to-face, and the coach is sensitive to verbal and vocal nuance, the value of an occasional phone session may be close to that of a session in person; further, the client's skills at discerning aural clues may be enhanced over time, because it is so central to telephone coaching.

The issues for *group* telephone coaching are more complex: much of the interactive value of the group is lost on the phone, because so much of our non-conscious communication relies on visual clues and cues; see 'Communication' in Chapter 3. The relational context of all learning relies greatly on the non-conscious communication outlined in chapter two and three, much of which is visual or kinaesthetic. On the telephone, we have only the audible components of a vast array of data; the degree of mutual understanding is limited by what is necessarily excluded, however skilled the coach. Further, the number of relationships involved, and varying degrees of aural skill on the part of the participants, affect coaching results.

It is not that nothing useful can be done by phone, particularly if there is no alternative, it is that so much is missing, particularly for visually oriented learners. As with individual telephone work, group telephone coaching or supervision works best where it is a supplement or alternative to regular face-to-face coaching. The participants and the coach/ supervisor can then use their fuller knowledge of each other to imagine (and then articulate and check out) the meanings of the vocal cues. Although this takes longer and flows less freely, it is valuable in itself.

Group telephone coaching

- Relies on audible components of communication
- Meaning should be checked out more explicitly than in face-to-face work
- Best when following face-to-face work
- Allows the coach to make use of 'live' note-taking to assist observation
- A useful supplement when meeting is impossible
- Best in smaller groups already well established.

Size of group is important. Four or five people in a telephone supervision group, working over time, develop some sense of each other's contributions, especially if they sometimes meet face-to-face. A telephone group with twenty members, and/or a shifting population, that has never met, will struggle to interact beyond superficial levels. Where there has been no face to face contact, reticence about taking risks, when unable to assess quickly and non-verbally what the reactions are, is simply too great for many people, who then 'play safe' and thus limit their own learning and contributions, thus also limiting other peoples'. Sensitive group coaches may be able to deduce a good deal from the voice, but group members may be less skilled, and their rate of learning is slower than in a face-to-face group.

Telephone coaching can develop members' sensitivity to aural clues, provided the group is small and regular enough to enable genuine interaction. Supervision groups perhaps most commonly use the telephone as a supplement to group meetings, and maybe this is no accident. These groups tend to be at the smaller end of the spectrum, typically three or four members with a supervisor. Smaller groups which already have established relationships do best on the phone, because their prior knowledge of each other is greater, and the relationships are fewer and so easier to 'read' from aural data alone.

For the group coach, working on the telephone offers one significant advantage over face-to-face coaching: you can use drawing and note-taking 'live' to assist your observation. Making a diagram or drawing of the group, say as a circle with a point for each member, helps the visually-oriented coach hold the group in mind. You can then note who is talking or silent, what emotions you sense and from whom, any 'pairing' (see 'The basic assumptions' in chapter 10) or recurring themes, and conversation flow, such as who typically follows whom, or who usually affirms or contradicts whom.

In the course of writing this book I googled 'group coaching'. I was intrigued to discover that what mostly came up was a series of teleconference opportunities, more or less baldly presented as a way of boosting the coach's income by 'coaching' large numbers of people remotely and in modest amounts of time. Such groups cannot meet the basic criterion for coaching, which is attention to the learning needs of individuals, since groups of 25–30 people who have never met and whose membership is constantly changing, cannot work at much depth in the space of 1–2 hours on the phone. These tele-rallies may generate learning and perhaps motivation or belief, but I do not believe that they are group telephone coaching.

Coaching sessions within management development programmes and other ongoing training groups

Coaching is not training. Longer training programmes can however incorporate group coaching sessions within their structure, providing an opportunity for the participants to take ownership of what they have learned. The coaching sessions should take place at every meeting of the training group, and should be set up as carefully as any other group coaching exercise. Ideally the trainers should not act as group coaches, to decrease the risk of role confusion.

- Have group coaching sessions at each meeting of the training group.
- Confidentiality – group coaches ideally not same people as trainers.
- Each person works on something that is their interpretation of the training material, not directed by coach or trainers (but open to challenge from the group).
- Continuity in coaching is easier if the training context provides in-depth exploration of material rather than 'a quilt of many tools', since the material in the taught sessions will often influence the coaching sessions.
- Small enough groups to allow each person to update on progress and think about overcoming obstacles each time – use 'turns'.
- Enough time.
- Methodology – can vary, but use something rigorous to keep the conversation focused.
- Agreed mechanism to feed back 'themes' or shared difficulties that have structural or organizational origins, without betraying individual confidentiality.

It is important for the coach to be scrupulous in ensuring that the members of the coaching groups retain individual control over their learning goals. The aim is to achieve an individual interpretation of what has been learned through the training. To get the benefit of the learning group method, individuals must be free to work on learning goals that are truly important to them.

Finally on learning groups: users' views of the interpersonal skill gains

I have recently (2006–2008) had the privilege of researching learning group processes,[125] where members were training as group coaches for action learning sets. They were eloquent about their gains:

- use of open questioning in work and life habits
- growth of self-awareness
- growth of understanding, confidence and skills as a group facilitator
- learning to ask better questions
- learning to challenge performance deficits such as poor questioning
- letting go of anxious control in a group situation
- self-restraint and pace: waiting and thinking before speaking
- managing the beginning of the group
- learning to say what hasn't been said.

In this chapter we have described four types of learning group. In the next, we focus on a fifth type, the supervision group. The material in that chapter, particularly about the reflection process (also known as parallel process), is also relevant to *all* learning groups.

Supervision groups

This chapter contains:

- This chapter
- The origins of coaching supervision, and group supervision theory
- Supervision and supervision groups
- Advantages and limitations of group supervision
- Managing competition and rivalry in the supervision group
- The reflection process
- The reflection process and supervision of groups
- The reflection process: beware
- Beginning a supervision group
- Structuring a supervision group
- Common supervisor errors
- What helps the supervision group work effectively?
- Presentation and its vicissitudes

This chapter

In the last chapter we introduced learning groups, and in this chapter we focus on a particular kind of learning group, the supervision group. This chapter presents a deeper insight into their dynamics, with particular attention to the 'reflection process' or 'parallel process', a powerful tool for understanding the coaching work presented. It discusses the dynamics of learning, how to handle competition, how to open and structure supervision groups, some common supervisor errors, and the characteristics of the effective supervisor; it considers presentation styles in supervision.

The origins of coaching supervision, and group supervision theory

Supervision is a mechanism for safeguarding quality of work, and developing professional skill and competence, adopted into coaching from the analogous professions of counselling, psychotherapy and social work. The most widely used models in supervising one-to-one coaching are adapted from the counselling field.[126] These books offer useful checklists and methods for managing the complexities of supervision, such as the 'seven-eye' model[127] and the 'helping/hindering' and 'structured group supervision model'[128] (which is similar to the Balint method described in the previous chapter). This chapter extends these discussions by focusing on the group dynamic dimension of supervision groups, and introducing ideas from a group-specific supervision literature.

In psychotherapy, supervision is sometimes wryly described as 'a practice in search of a theory',[129] and indeed the basic model is one of apprenticeship with little attention to individual learning styles. The models developed are practice-oriented; Bernard and Goodyear[130] give a good account. The development of supervision theory has been slow, the single and outstanding exception being Searles' discovery of the reflection process.[131] In the past fifteen years, as supervision has been understood to be a distinct professional activity, the body of analytic theory has begun to grow.[132]

While group supervision is common, it is 'widely practiced but little understood'.[133] Group analysis offers a literature of elaborated group supervision practice, but this literature is not widely known among individually qualified practitioners, and development of theory has also been slow. We need supervision theory and group theory to be melded into a properly elaborated theory of group supervision. The approach described in this chapter is primarily from a group-analytic supervision perspective.

Supervision and supervision groups

Here is a definition of supervision.

> Supervision is a relationship in which the practitioner can reflect on and develop her/his practice and understanding in her/his client work.

Supervision benefits the client and the coach, or, more exactly, the client through the greater integration of the coach's knowledge and practice skills: in supervision, coaches can integrate theory with practice.

Supervision *groups* offer multiple relationships in which the practitioner can undertake this reflection. Their primary purpose is to help the coach members with their client work, and so contribute to their development as reflective professionals. Supervision groups are particularly valuable in supervising group and team coaching, because their dynamics can more fully mirror the dynamics in the work.

In a supervision group, each member has the experience of being supervised, and of supervising as a member of the group, with the capacity of the supervisor to understand augmented by the capacities of all the others, who participate in both ways. The supervisor also has a triple role, nurturing the individual members, and the group's capacity to work effectively, while attending to the work presented. The fluidity of role makes supervision groups more effective than individual supervision at developing confidence and independence alongside competence.

Supervision groups are in essence learning groups, and all the advantages that accrue from ongoing learning groups apply to them: they broaden and enrich learning, by engaging in depth with others' work, strengthen interpersonal sensitivity and provide a multiple sounding board generating a range of alternative strategies and styles of feedback. They are fundamentally more egalitarian than one-to-one supervision, particularly when the coaches in the group are themselves experienced. The supervisor is part of the group too, a kind of 'first among equals' bringing greater experience and training to the table. The supervisor's ability to 'hold' the group's learning is central.[134] See Chapter 2 for a full discussion of holding.

The conscious wish to collaborate and learn through supervision is balanced, and sometimes frustrated, by the unconscious wish to avoid the discomfort of learning. All supervision poses some challenge for the supervisee, because of the inherent risk of exposure. In describing the difficulties we find in our professional work, we risk feeling ashamed; we can fear that others will criticize or think less well of us if we relate the things of which we are least sure about ourselves.

This underlying dynamic influences whether we choose individual or group supervision, though the decision cuts both ways. Some prefer the privacy of individual supervision since it limits to one the number of other people who might be critical, albeit one in a more hierarchical position. Others prefer the group, since most of the time the spotlight is on others so one can quietly learn, and since any impasse with the supervisor can be mediated by the other group members.[135] In either setting, the supervisee must find adequate holding to enable the possibility of learning.

Like action learning sets and Balint groups, supervision groups usually rely on turn-taking. The superficial process may seem deceptively simple, as each member in turn presents an aspect of their work for collective reflection, but these are groups with a peculiar complexity of underlying process. The coach supervisor is attending to the needs of the supervisee presenting, of the group, and to the piece of work being presented. S/he is holding the focus of the group, assisting each member with the client work presented, to the forefront, in the face of many fascinating alternatives.

Some ideas about supervision

- 'The slightest thing – a remark, an image, an attitude, a word – is a possible golden opportunity'[136]
- Features of the coaching relationship are likely to enter the supervisory relationship
- Group reverie reaches deeper levels of meaning to facilitate change
- New ways of thinking and working are best introduced in a practical, practice-oriented way.

If s/he is analytically trained, her/his attention is hovering between the conscious and unconscious communications presented in the work, and to be deduced in the group, so as to surface the fullest possible picture of 'what is really going on'.

Advantages and limitations of group supervision

Bernard and Goodyear (2009) list nine advantages of group supervision compiled from various sources: economies of time, costs and expertise; opportunities for vicarious learning; breadth of client exposure; more diverse feedback; more understandable feedback (because supervisees speak each other's language better than does the 'expert' supervisor); a more rounded supervisor picture of each supervisee (through observation in different interactions); learning supervision skills; normalizing experiences; and the particular value of the reflection process in supervising work with teams and groups.

The limitations are charted by Carroll,[137] and include the possibility of supervisees receiving insufficient time and attention; disruption of work through rivalry and competition; overload; inappropriate use of supervision time. The supervisor can address and minimize all these through astute and assertive leadership. An active stance is needed, in structuring the group, setting the right tone, articulating what is needed, and challenging departures from desired group norms.

In addition to these, the usefulness of supervision can be limited by a failure to engage with the implications of diversity in the group; for example, if a mainly female coach supervision group contains one man, or a white european supervisor works with a group entirely composed of coaches from other cultures. In these circumstances, to hold the group effectively and be sensitive to the impact of seen and felt differences, the coach supervisor must be aware of the broader implications of her/his position, and curious, willing to question and learn across cultures and other difference divides. See further 'Exchange' in Chapter 2.

Managing competition and rivalry in the supervision group

Managing time effectively (see 'Structuring a supervision group' below) and managing feelings of competition and rivalry are two critical supervisor skills. Supervision groups naturally stir up feelings of competition, as members compare themselves to each other and ask such questions as 'Who is the best coach?', 'Who cares most about their clients?', 'Who has the most difficult cases?', 'Who is most insightful?'.[138] This is normal enough, and can lead to an atmosphere of healthy competition if handled well. The first and most important step is for the supervisor to let members know that s/he has noticed it. The aim is to bring these dynamics into conscious awareness. It is also important for the supervisor to comment early on signs of over-rivalrous behaviour, such as putting other members down. Inhibition in presentation may indicate fear of being attacked, and the supervisor does well to enquire (gently), particularly if an individual's ability to present seems weaker than usual. See also 'Competition, envy and admiration' in Chapter 4.

If one or more members are competing with the supervisor, perhaps to show how much better they are at supervising, it is important that the supervisor does not enter the competition. It is also important that s/he does not let the challenge pass unmarked. A good route can be to summarize the comments made and invite other perspectives alongside: this underlines the importance of the multiple perspectives of the group, and lets the challenger know that the challenge was noticed, without a put-down. If competitive contributions come too fast to allow time for thought, the supervisor should step in to restore the working norms of the group. Making the unconscious competition conscious is the aim of the supervisor here.

The reflection process[139]

Vignette: Reflection process 1

The coach presented a client's great perplexity about how to proceed. The client is founder CEO of a technical company, whose success is founded on innovation. Competition from companies manufacturing in Asia will reduce profitability steadily over the next five years, and he is faced with a dilemma: move manufacturing to a less expensive environment, which will not ensure growth, and will result in over 1000 redundancies locally, or risk persisting with local production in the hope that further innovation will retain the company's market-leading position.

The coach explains the contradictions faced by the client, gets confused and contradicts himself, all the while speaking faster and faster. The group feel confused and powerless, and at the same time greatly burdened with a need to help.

The supervisor asks how what is happening here and now in the group relates to what the coach is presenting, which helps the group members express their helplessness and bewilderment. Some discover that their feelings reflect the coach's feelings of being paralysed by the scale of the decision, and unable to help his client, which in turn reflect the client's feelings about his responsibilities to his staff.

One member expresses irritation at the coach's apparent panic. The coach comments that he felt angry with himself. Another, an entrepreneur with business failures as well as successes in her past, is attuned to the magnitude of the stakes – 'playing God with people's lives'. She sees how this had paralysed the coach as it paralysed the client, and in turn paralysed the supervision group. Once the feelings of impotence and the fear of power had been explored, the coach was able to re-establish the reflective relationship with his client.

This is a relatively simple example of how the reflection process – sometimes called parallel process – works in a supervision group. The client's feelings that paralyse him are communicated unconsciously to the coach, who then communicates them to the group, including the supervisor. Words are only a small part of the communication: tone, pace and gesture communicate the emotional content of the dilemma (see 'Communication' in Chapter 3). Different members of the group held different parts of the puzzle, according to their own predilections and experiences.

How is it that these competent professionals (all the way up the chain) were temporarily so gripped by these primitive emotions? It is because the strength of the feelings provoked and *unconsciously* communicated is mirrored and amplified in the experience of the hearers – they resonate in the group. All could feel some part of the emotion communicated. Used consciously, this amplification is a unique strength of group supervision. By fully experiencing the problem and then, in response to the supervisor's enquiry, regaining the capacity to reflect, the group was able to contain the coach's panic and so the client's. Group members also learned something about the impact of such apparently normal business decisions, and how to work with them, through the reflection process.

What would have happened if the link between the material and the feelings in the group had not been spotted? We can't know for certain, but it is likely that members and/ or supervisor would have been left feeling frustrated, with a sense of 'unfinished business', and the presenting coach would not so soon have recovered his confidence.

In the example, some members identified with the coach's frozen state and some reacted against it. The identification was unconscious, and members responded according to their own normal patterns. In the face of powerlessness, some of us are paralysed by panic and some 'get busy' – whether or not the activity truly addresses the dilemma that raised the feelings of helplessness. We could present the reactions to the discomfort of helpless feelings on a scale.

'There's nothing I can do'   'I'm in charge, must act!'

←—————————————————————————————→

The dilemma of dependence versus independence is brought sharply into focus in supervision groups,[140] as group members work to make sense of their relationship to the supervisor and to the others in the group. This is particularly true in a training situation.

The example illustrates the working of the reflection process, where the emotional dynamics experienced in the work presented are reflected among those present as the work is recounted. This is also sometimes called 'parallel process'.

Individual supervision is a complex undertaking with twelve possible axes of communication (taking account of the conscious and unconscious parts of the three people involved, client, coach and supervisor, gives the twelve axes).[141] The reflection process operates through the medium of the coach's relationships with both client and supervisor.

The diagrams below represent a supervision group of

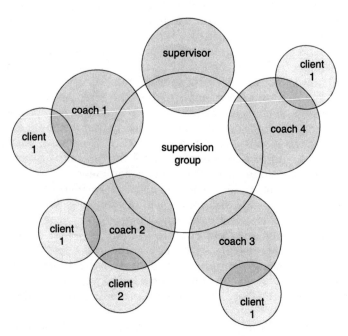

Supervision group supervising individual coaching

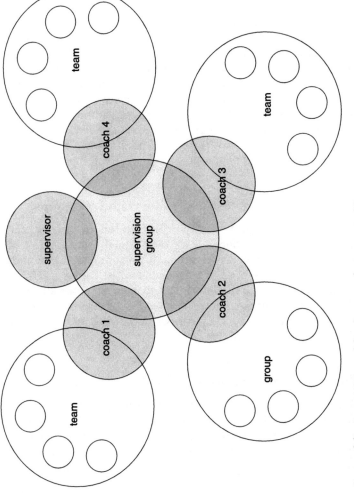

Supervision group supervising team and group coaching

one supervisor and four coaches. Where one client each is presented, we could add an overlapping circle to each of the four coach's circles. In the first diagram, three coaches present one client each and one coach (Coach 2) presents two clients.

Where the supervision is in a group, the possibilities for communication, conscious and unconscious, increase by a factor for each additional person in the group, and where the work supervised is *with* a team or a group, it multiplies again. Its complexity can be seen in the second diagram, where each coach presents a team or group of four. It is the power of the reflection process that helps us first surface the dynamics, and then, through use of careful reflection on our responses, select the most relevant and develop a hypothesis to guide the coach's next steps.

The reflection process and supervision of groups

Although this sounds highly complicated in theory, the reflection process offers an extraordinarily fine degree of focus on the issues. As each coach presents, the dynamics of the group presented are experienced in the supervision group. As this is articulated, it becomes possible for what was previously unconscious to come into consciousness and be thought about, so that conscious choices can be made about focus and strategies.

The reflection process: beware

When first working with the reflection process, it is not uncommon to be captivated by its remarkable power to illuminate previously unthought of aspects of a situation. Supervisors can easily be seduced into assuming an unwarranted degree of certainty about their interpretations. Beware.

The reflection process needs to be used thoughtfully. The process twists and turns through the psyches of many people on its route to the supervision group; its expression in the supervision group will include distortions arising from the perspectives of each member of the group, including the supervisor.[142]

While it sheds strong light on the problem presented, the mirroring is not exact, as the vignette below shows. What it does reflect accurately is the underlying *feeling* that is unable to be thought about, the obstacle to progress.

Vignette: Reflection process 2

Frank was working with a college English Department, whose Head, Aggie, was very anxious. The department had gone through a very bad patch and pupils were consistently achieving lower grades than they should, based on their previous performance. As the team coaching progressed, Aggie became increasingly agitated and spent a good proportion of her one-to-one sessions asking Frank whether there was something he could do to move things along faster. Frank felt irritated and undermined. The Head Teacher, a calm man who had commissioned the work, withdrew once it began. 'No wonder, to get away from Aggie!' commented one of the supervision group. Everyone laughed, including Frank and the supervisor.

The supervisor found himself thinking about the laughter, and its contrast with the serious consequences of the team's failures for its pupils. Aggie's distress seemed more understandable. The men in the group had laughed the hardest, and he found himself wondering whether gender was part of the issue. He asked the men what Frank's tale had stirred in them. With some reticence, one spoke of his fear of powerful women, and another agreed.

Frank leaned forward. He spoke of his discomfort working with the mainly female English team, and of his fantasy of running away from Aggie. Thinking out loud, it became clear to Frank that his anger was interfering with his ability to coach Aggie and engage with her concerns. Although her anxiety was annoying, it arose from her frustration. Aggie had gone into teaching out of a sense that she had got her life chances through education, and wanted to 'give something back' to students from poor backgrounds like her own. She had a sense of the urgency of the problem that the rest of the team had not fully 'got'. Frank had not got it either, till now, as he reflected on the long-term impact for students of poor results in English. Frank had been over-identified with the team, at the expense of Aggie's genuine concern for the students.

To aid the fluent use of parallel process, the supervisor can encourage a kind of group reverie[143] or free association to the material presented. Group members are encouraged to listen quietly to the presenter, paying attention to their internal responses – fantasies, memories and thoughts – and then to choose something to share. Group members' comments have the purpose neither of supporting nor criticizing the presenter, but simply of opening up a new angle. Group reverie has some common ground with the Balint method described in the previous chapter. The impact of each person sharing their responses without judgement can illuminate previously unnoticed aspects of the case, and, as the group matures, builds a common language and way of working together.

The reflection process affects all supervision groups to some degree, and it is helpful for supervisors to bear it in mind, even where it is not used as a primary tool in supervision. Where ignored, it can disrupt and undermine supervision. To work with it, the supervisor needs training in working with awareness of unconscious dynamics. It will often take some time for a new supervision group to develop skill in working at this level, even if some of the coaches are similarly trained. The reflection process will be at work, but a new group needs to become accustomed to working with each other on the irrational and inexplicable. The power to illuminate coaching dilemmas of this way of working provides the motivation, but the capacity can only develop through use.

For very anxious groups or for less experienced practitioners, the method has some pitfalls. Using personal reactions in this way requires members to have a personal maturity, and an ability to distinguish between exploration in the service of improving client work (supervision) and of personal growth (therapy). Having had some experience of personal therapy certainly helps members keep the boundaries clear, but it is the supervisor's role to help the group stay within them.

Beginning a supervision group

Any supervision group begins with the contact between the supervisor and potential group members, when it is important to discuss what the supervisee's goals are from supervision, and what s/he expects it to be like. Each person should meet the supervisor individually before the first group session. The supervisor should select members with enough homogeneity as regards length of experience to create a reasonably balanced group, and enough heterogeneity of experience to make a wide variety of viewpoints available to the group. Since irregular attendance disrupts the work of the group, the supervisor should emphasize the importance of regularly being there.

The first meeting of a supervision group has much in common with the first meeting of any other group in terms of what members need (see 'Setting a new group up right – the first meeting' in Chapter 11). It is important for the supervisor to establish conditions conducive to openness and learning, so that the group can become a secure base to tackle the theoretical and ethical dilemmas of client work. S/he should state what s/he hopes the group to achieve, model the kind of behaviour s/he wishes to see, and encourage the group members to express their goals.

As with coaching, there should be an explicit, preferably written contract, discussed beforehand with prospective members of the group and confirmed at the first meeting. The text box shows headings to consider for a group supervision contract.

Checklist for group supervision contracts

- What is the purpose of the group?
- How many people are involved?
- When, how frequent and how long are the sessions?
- What is the structure of the sessions and what are the presentation guidelines?
- What are the expectations about attendance and arrangements for setting dates?
- What happens about cancelled, missed or late sessions?
- What are the fees?
- What does this way of working require of group members?
- What are the confidentiality requirements?
- How to deal with emergencies?
- What are the expectations about insurance or communicating with others besides the client, including the sponsoring organization?
- How might material from supervision be used, and how will consent be sought?
- What records are kept?
- What notice is expected of termination?

Structuring a supervision group

In the counselling and therapeutic contexts from which coaching supervision is derived, supervision happens relatively frequently, particularly during training and the early years of practice, with the interval lengthening as experience grows. It is not uncommon for supervision groups to meet weekly. This is relatively uncommon among coaches, where monthly meeting is more usual. The longer interval results in a longer lead-in time to achieve the cohesion and group confidence that create an effective working group, and challenges the supervisor to create a climate and structures promoting both.

In structuring a monthly supervision group, it is important to ensure that everyone has some opportunity to speak about their work on each occasion. It is simplest to do this by allocating everyone a slot of equal length, as in other kinds of learning groups. Some groups, particularly of newer coaches, also keep some time in reserve for emergencies. In groups meeting more frequently, such as weekly groups, an equal time slot is less important, but the supervisor must keep an eye on the distribution of time to ensure equity.

Some groups negotiate time at each meeting, but in a monthly group this is a tricky undertaking, because of the competitive feelings it can stir up, and the symbolic meaning of some getting more than others. It requires an alert and tenacious supervisor. There is a risk too that such a process merely confirms some members' subjective sense that theirs is a really big problem (or for some people, really small, not deserving of time).

In many years conducting and participating in supervision groups, I have observed that given equal time slots and a rigorously observed time limit, progress can be made in most cases. It is as though members internalize the length of time they have, and manage to get what they need within it.

When members do not get what they need, extending the time will not necessarily alter that fact; the (uncomfortable) function of supervision on these occasions is to confirm the stuckness the coach has brought. Rather than extend the slot, it is better to review it, in the manner of the 'thoughts unuttered, feelings unexpressed' check described in Chapter 7. This allows the issue to be faced, allows the presenter to get some further feedback that may be useful in unsticking things, and the group to process its feelings of frustration, etc. The stuckness can be worked on, rather than extending its re-enactment in the original slot, or confirming a sense that this is a 'special' problem.

Monthly supervision groups are usually smaller groups, with around four members. The reasons for this are generally pragmatic, to do with the time available divided by the time needed for each person to have a substantial 'turn'. Supervision groups are therefore properly limited to a size that allows each member a reasonable amount of time in which to focus on their work. Half an hour per person is a good rule of thumb, though I like to add an extra half-hour (so that a four member + supervisor group meets for 2.5 hours) for collective reflection, and to allow the group to finish comfortably on time.

Common supervisor errors

- Being too silent or too talkative
- Being too solemn or too inattentive to real points beneath flippancy
- Not balancing attention to the work with attention to the individuals
- Not balancing attention to the work with attention to the group
- Agreeing to be 'the expert on all things'
- Allowing the focus of the group to be skewed
- Ignoring differences in response to individual members
- Failing to balance appreciation and criticism
- Suppressing the group's involvement in supervising.

Being too silent or too talkative

Like the reactions to powerlessness shown in the scale in 'The reflection process' above, anxiety is the common source of these two apparently opposing supervisor errors. Supervisors may say too little out of a desire to appear wise (or at least, in common with supervisees, out of a desire not to appear foolish!). This can be particularly unhelpful early in the life of a supervision group, when the members are observing the supervisor's behaviour closely to see how they are expected to act. The supervisor should be modelling the calm and thoughtful curiosity that s/he wishes members to display, while also actively promoting the group members' learning. It may also be unhelpful to be silent at anxious moments in the group, when things feel fraught. This is a matter of degree and of the group's maturity. It is good to let members struggle with the discomforts of uncertainty, but not good to let them drown in unreasoning panic.

Talking too much is a more obviously anxious response, often related to the supervisor lacking confidence in the group's capacity and feeling that s/he needs to 'make it work', or to control things. S/he may feel that s/he needs personally to 'give value' by offering the most profound insights, and may fail to see the competitiveness of needing always to be 'the expert'. Working effectively in a group depends on faith in the group to pursue its task competently, given a little light guidance.

Being too solemn or too inattentive to real points beneath flippancy

Because something is serious business is no reason not to laugh about it. We do not need to be solemn in order to be serious about our work, and seeing the funny side puts us in touch with our common humanity, sometimes in the face of what is truly tragic. We need humour to aid our learning and to make connections with each other.

On the other hand, we have all had group experiences where humour is defensive, where something very difficult is discounted – not-quite-faced – through an appeal to humour. The competent supervisor draws attention to the 'true words spoken in jest' and helps the group to work with the real dilemma.

Not balancing attention to the work with attention to the individuals

As the group matures and uses its emotional and intellectual intelligence with greater and greater precision in the service of the work, the desire to use those resources to solve more personal problems may be strong. There is always a tension between focusing on the work and focusing on the coach doing the work. Sometimes a supervision group needs to help a member see through a personal blind spot, but if it *always* focuses there, it has probably crossed a line into becoming a surreptitious therapy group. On the other hand, if the focus on the work is so tight that the person in the role is *never* considered, the work will be impoverished and will sometimes entirely miss critical learning points.

Not balancing attention to the work with attention to the group

Although the focus of the work is on the coaching, at times the communications about the work will also have direct relevance to the group. It is a mistake to ignore this; often a simple acknowledgement of the parallels will be enough to free up communication. For example, a charismatic supervisor on a training programme left suddenly, and was replaced in the group by a supervisor whom none of the group knew. The very first case presented was about a client who experienced his boss as a wicked stepmother.

Agreeing to be 'the expert on all things'

Some coaches are prone to idealize their supervisors, seeing them as the fount of all knowledge, wisdom and experience, in contrast to their own sense of confusion and 'not knowing how to do it'. This is a particular issue on training courses, and particularly in the early stages.

For some supervisors, this can be a seductive experience. Who would not want to be so important and full of expertise? Well, the wise and experienced supervisor would not. Even where the skills gap is genuinely great, the role of the supervisor is gently to nurture confidence and independence in group members. To stay in a permanently superior position robs supervisees of part of their own competence, and fails in the supervisory role of nurturing independence and the development of the 'internal supervisor'.[144]

The kind of split described, where the supervisees' self-denigration is counterbalanced by an overestimate of the supervisor's abilities, is a kind of projection. Supervisees, at the outset of a new learning experience, are necessarily very focused on what they *don't* know, and often lose sight of their own abilities and project or 'give' them all to the supervisor. Their task is to regain them, so as to become confident in their own abilities. The supervisor's task is to encourage this process. The group is a splendid medium for this process, because (when it works well) the psychological concept moves from 'good supervisor' to 'good-group-of-which-I-am-a-part' to 'I am a good coach'. The disowned confidence (sense of having abilities) is recovered through the medium of the group (see 'Connectedness and belonging' in Chapter 4).

Allowing the focus of the group to be skewed

It can be difficult at times for supervision groups to retain a clear focus. Their work sits on various boundaries, between the client's interests and the coach's, between the coaches' work and their blind spots, between theory and practice, between training and achieving qualified status.

In supervision groups on a training course, fear may inhibit what members present – 'if I say that, I will fail the course' – or supervisees may have an exaggerated deference (or rebelliousness) towards the supervisor as an authority figure.

The focus of the group needs to be fluid in order to be creative, moving from what is presented to what is going on in the group to the individual presenting, and back again. Members will become caught up in discussing the presenter's client as though s/he were their client. If the client is not 'handed back' to the presenter s/he may feel robbed or denigrated by this process.

This is just one of the ways in which the process can become skewed, with the gratification of individuals interfering with the work. Others include focusing on the client work and never considering the individuals carrying out the work, focusing on individual 'therapy', or becoming so fascinated by the group dynamics that the group's task gets lost. It is the supervisor's role to keep the group task in mind at all times, and to refocus group members on that when necessary. This will often require the supervisor to intervene actively.

Ignoring differences in response to individual members

The members of a supervision group are individuals, as is the supervisor. S/he will warm to some characteristics and to some people, and dislike aspects of others. The supervisor must maintain a self-disciplined awareness of these responses, and be thoughtful about how to use these responses in the work. If s/he fails to do so, s/he for example may 'play favourites', focus on some people more than others, be harsher with some supervisees than others, or handle time boundaries unfairly.

Failing to balance appreciation and criticism

We have seen from Chapter 2 that to learn, we need to have a balance between feeling secure and the opportunity for exploration. The supervisor should neither over-use nor neglect to express appreciation. It must be sincere and well targeted. See 'Encouragement' in Chapter 4. If a supervisor is feeling critical of a supervisee's work, the safest line to pursue is one of enquiry. This gives the supervisee the opportunity to self-correct, and the group to offer alternative strategies. Reasoning about the best styles of intervention can be encouraged.

Vignette: Anxiety and irritation

As Helena presented her session with Anna, the supervisor felt irritated by how mechanical the work seemed. Helena described how hard she had had to work to stay 'in "coaching" mode' in the face of Anna's rising irritation; since Anna had asked for direct feedback, the supervisor could understand her feelings. The rest of the group was silent, and the supervisor struggled for a useful question to ask Helena. 'What did her irritation make you feel?' allowed Helena to acknowledge a panicky feeling that the session was going wrong and she didn't know what to do. This had led her to stick even tighter to a 'non-directive' style. Anna had commented at the end of the session that she hadn't made progress, and had cancelled the next session. Another group member commented that when she was nervous she also became rather rigid and so she felt for Helena.

'How else might we handle that?' produced a discussion ranging from options for managing anxious internal states to different ways of engaging with the client. Helena commented that she had gained much food for thought about what coaching really was.

The pattern of anxiety and irritation from the coaching session reappeared in supervision, with the supervisor experiencing the client's feelings. An enquiring approach enabled Helena to learn without further loss of face.

Suppressing the group's involvement in supervising

As the group supervisor, beware of always having the first, or the last, word. The purpose of the supervisor is to make the group containing and safe enough for the *group* to supervise the members. At times your greater experience will be of great use to members, but it will not be in every single presentation. The value of the group is in the rich picture developed through members' diverse responses; further, for the development of supervisees, the experience of helping others is at least as important as being helped.

What helps the supervision group work effectively?

In a paper written jointly by a training supervisor and supervisees,[145] it was found that a fundamentally open and supportive style on the part of the group supervisor, as a 'colleague in a leadership role', together with a firm focus on the task of learning from the work:

- reduced the impact of negative and fearful transferences about authority
- enabled students to relate more openly to each other as colleagues
- created a culture of working together openly and supportively on the task
- reduced the tendency to project all expertise into the supervisor
- kept the focus on the client work.

It is noteworthy that this successful supervision group was conducted by a supervisor experienced not only in supervision, but in working with groups. Some supervision courses require trainees to supervise in groups, without providing the needed training or support in group skills. A training in individual supervision is valuable in understanding what is happening in a group, but it is not sufficient to equip the supervisor for the range of challenges s/he will face in 'using the group in all its interactive complexity as it resonates in a myriad ways to aspects of a case'.[146]

The supervision style described in this chapter is most achievable by the experienced and group-trained supervisor working with relatively experienced coaches.[147] Less experienced coaches – or supervisors – may need a firmer style of leadership at first, before experiencing sufficient safety to take up this more creative style of working. It can nevertheless be achieved to some degree with most groups, by a supervisor who is willing to be curious, fallible and responsive to the need of her/his group.

Presentation and its vicissitudes

Presenting in supervision is an important skill in itself, and our natural style will reflect our personalities. Some are anxious, halting speakers; some are natural raconteurs, telling the story with wit and style; some present painstaking blow-by-blow accounts, based on meticulous process notes; some work around key moments or interactions. Whatever the natural style, we can all improve our presentation, and the supervisor can make a contribution by encouraging experimentation.

Presentation of work in supervision is a memory and representation of the work done, not the work actually done. This is true even when we use audiovisual recording, since although there is an accurate record of content, this cannot reproduce the internal experiences of coach and client. Bernard and Goodyear[148] offer a valuable review of the issues in using technological, observational and interventionist methods of supervision.

Most supervision still relies on the memory and records kept by the supervisee, and 'works best if [we] remain aware that what [we] are jointly imagining is not true'.[149] That is, it is one perspective on what is true, and at a remove. A painting of a field of poppies is not the same thing as a field of poppies, but paint on canvas.[150] This is exactly analogous to supervision, where the client describes her/his experiences to the coach who describes in supervision her/his experience of hearing these disclosures, with the aim of understanding them better and working with them more effectively. Remembering that the experience in supervision is somewhat removed from the client's experience, notwithstanding the power of parallel process in recreating some elements, keeps us humble in our ideas about 'what really happened'.

Helping coaches to present better is nevertheless a worthwhile endeavour, because it also helps them to remember better what they have heard and observed during their coaching sessions. Good observation is a prerequisite of good understanding, even if what is observed does not immediately fit any available theory. Recordings alongside memory are helpful in highlighting the 'forgotten' aspects of an interaction, which may hold important clues. Where recordings are not used, there are many ways of remembering, and a group session is more difficult to remember than an individual session.

Ways of remembering a group coaching session[151]

- *Visual/pictorial.* Who sat where in the group supervised, how people looked; strong images from the session
- *Aural.* The kinds of language used, the intonation and volume of speech; other sounds
- *Kinetic.* Communications through physical movement, orientation or gesture
- *Emotional/relational.* How group members related to each other, feelings in the room, how they changed during the session
- *Thematic.* An account of main themes in the session and how group members related to them
- *Critical incidents.* Key events in the session, particularly disturbing the boundaries of the session, reactions to them
- *Chronology.* A blow-by-blow account of what happened.

The better coaches remember their coaching work, the more likely the supervision session is to get close to the important issues. For coaches without perfect memories, therefore, some form of recording or note-taking is essential.

Once coaches have begun to experiment with ways of remembering the work, it is useful also to experiment with different ways of presenting the work in supervision. This allows the group to offer something accessible to coaches with a variety of learning styles, and helps everyone diversify their options. Here are some possibilities.

Ways of presenting in supervision

- *Process account.* A blow-by-blow chronological account of what happened, with feelings/visuals/ movements, etc. recorded in the margin alongside
- *Single issue.* Focusing on all the examples of one behaviour, such as lateness
- *Spontaneous report.* For more confident and experienced coaches – setting all notes aside and reporting from memory. Can be compared with notes later. Good for training memory
- *Focusing on an individual.* Useful when one member of the coaching group or team presented is stuck, or may drop out. Reviewing all available data about that person to achieve a fuller understanding of her/ his position
- *Role-play.* An account of the group session and members of the supervision group role-play it, while the presenting coach sits outside and observes; discussion follows. Useful with larger supervision groups. Can be varied by stopping the action for discussion at key points
- *Theoretical analysis.* The presenter focuses on a particular theoretical concept s/he wishes to understand more fully, such as transference or resonance, and presents material from the coaching session in the light of the concept
- *Brainstorming.* A problem is presented and everyone offers spontaneous associations and ideas, without trying to guide or judge the presenter.

This completes our review of learning groups and Part 4 of the book. Part 5 offers practical advice on running groups, beginning in the next chapter by reviewing strategies for dealing with members' problematic behaviour.

Part 5

Part 5

Strategies for tackling problem behaviour

This chapter

This chapter is concerned with tackling, as it arises in the moment, behaviour that disrupts the work of the group. 'Problem' behaviour offers teams golden opportunities for learning. We consider how to deal with anger, distress, domination, silence, and other challenges. The additional learning opportunities for a team are described fully in the section on dealing with anger, and can then be inferred for the remaining topics.

When a highly task-focused team cannot collaborate

Problem behaviour provides individual learning opportunities in any group, but for a team there is the added

This chapter contains:

- This chapter
- When a highly task-focused group cannot collaborate
- Process breaks and process skills
- Developing skilful discussion
- Dealing with overt anger in a group
- Holding the group or team through conflict and struggle
- When someone is crying or distressed
- Dealing with people who are dominating
- When someone is silent or over-quiet
- When someone is playing 'yes but'
- When someone's contribution is always boring
- When someone cannot acknowledge anything but logic
- When someone is so self-centred they cannot work on the task

benefit of having their dynamics worked with 'live'. Even very task-focused groups can be persuaded of the value of understanding their team dynamic better, when their work is disrupted by problem behaviour. With teams resistant to the idea that collaboration is a necessary work skill, use problem behaviour as an opportunity to educate them. Working with these issues may reveal more complex underlying problems. See further 'Dealing with unspoken expectations and dynamics' in Chapter 6 and 'Working with unconscious and unspoken conflicts' and 'Working with conflicting messages' in Chapter 10.

Process breaks and process skills

A process break allows a team or group time out to review *how* they are working together to achieve the task as well as working directly on the task. Use it with teams who need to communicate more openly, and invoke it when something seems to be getting in the way of the task, either something unspoken or some eruption of apparently inapposite emotion.

The process break gives teams permission to speak about and make use of emotional and non-conscious information (see 'Communication' in Chapter 3), and so is a useful device in training them to do so. If necessary, stress that it is in the service of the task.

As teams develop more robust communication, the process break more rarely needs to be invoked. In a team that has learned to value fuller feedback as part of its collaboration on shared tasks, it becomes automatic to share thoughts and feelings in the course of the work, including sharing questions and disagreement in a robust way.

With task-focused groups, simple conceptual frameworks can spell out what is involved in collaborating effectively, or underline its importance. The box shows one, a simple but flexible collaboration framework with many uses. It sets out desirable collaborative behaviour when engaged in a group discussion task. Some points are directly task-directed, and some help the task by improving group process.

Working together effectively	
Activities that forward the task directly	**Activities that forward the task by sustaining the group**
• Defining the issue and summarizing • Questioning and clarifying • Asking for/giving information • Making suggestions • Discussing pros and cons of suggestions • Testing relevance.	• Testing for consensus • Encouraging participation • Acknowledging others' contributions • Releasing tension, expressing feeling • Mediating.

This tool can be used in several ways to educate task-oriented groups in the value of attention to process in forwarding the task. Use it early in the coaching relationship to set parameters. It can be used as a tool within process breaks. It can be shared with a group at the start of a session, and used for a group evaluation towards the end. Using the simple form overleaf, you can set up a 'fishbowl' exercise with part of the group participating in the discussion and part observing, with a plenary discussion to improve understanding of the behaviours. You can use it over several sessions to focus on improving collaboration skills.

Developing skilful discussion

Another set of ideas that may help in these circumstances, particularly with very assertive and competitive groups, is Senge's[152] idea of *skilful discussion*. It usefully emphasizes the value of a questioning stance in improving the quality of decisions and goal achievement.

Skilful discussion is predicated on *dialogue*, a reflective conversation aiming at a meeting of minds, not simply

TASK ANALYSIS

TIME/PERSON	Defining the issue or objective	Summarizing and clarifying	Asking for/ giving information	Making suggestions	Discussing pros and cons of suggestions

GROUP SUSTAINING ANALYSIS

TIME/PERSON	Testing for consensus	Encouraging participation	Supporting others' contributions	Expressing feeling, releasing tension	Mediating

Tool for group observation

discharging a role: exploration, not decision, is the objective of dialogue. See also the discussion of large group dialogue in Chapter 5. Skilful discussion allows people to bring some of the qualities of a dialogue to a decision-making process, particularly an easy pace and genuine curiosity about the views of others (as opposed to relentless advocacy of one's own views).

Essential to skilful discussion are enough time, the ability to stay with uncertainty, and each person bringing their unique perspective to bear. The quality of interaction, rather than getting through business as quickly as possible, is crucial.

The obstacles to collaboration may go deeper than a simple non-awareness of its processes. If it becomes clear that a group cannot simply learn these new skills, then you are getting nearer the organizational dilemmas crippling it. See 'Dealing with unspoken expectations and dynamics' in Chapter 6 and 'Working with unconscious and unspoken conflicts' and 'Working with conflicting messages' in Chapter 10.

Dealing with overt anger in a group

Anger in the group presents a technical challenge for the coach, in balancing the usefulness of members tolerating a wider range of expressed feeling and maintaining or restoring a sense of safety. There is no single correct approach, because the most appropriate course will depend on the maturity of the group and the tolerance of its individual members for angry behaviour in others. Whatever the situation, however, the opportunity for everyone to express their reactions is central and must not be skipped over.

The coach must use her/his sense of what will work best with this particular team or group, but must also be prepared to act authentically and with authority. Some kinds of angry expression are beyond the acceptable, and the coach must back those who challenge the crossing of a line, or take the lead in doing so if the group members do not.

In dealing with anger in a group or team, there are two distinct stages. The first is to contain the explosion, and allow the angry person time to cool down. Engaging in

debate or reasoning is likely to lead to a row. The first objective is to allow the anger to run its course and get the group to
the point where members can again engage constructively
with each other. Only once in twenty-five years have I needed
to ask someone angry to leave the room for a while, but it is
helpful to remember that this is an option. More likely is
that the angry person will spontaneously leave, and that the
group will need help to decide how to deal with that.

The second stage is to help the group learn from the
experience so as to move on and return to task. A central
question is how the anger relates to the task.

Immediately

- *Take the time.* Accept that to deal with the anger will take
  time. Give up other objectives for the moment.
- *Hear them out.* Do not try to shut up a very angry person;
  to listen silently for a while can often allow the anger to
  run its course. When you judge that the angry person has
  become responsive again, ask a question to allow the discussion to start.
- *Forbid abuse.* If the person becomes abusive to you or
  someone else, challenge the abuse. Be careful to challenge
  the abusive behaviour, not the angry feeling or the angry
  person. If behaviour is excessive, you can ask them to
  leave to cool down.
- *Do not touch.* Do not touch the person or invade her/his
  physical space.
- *Listen and acknowledge.* Listen carefully. Acknowledge
  the anger by feeding back what is conveyed, including the
  feelings. When anger is heard, the need to express it
  diminishes somewhat.
- *Be realistic.* Facts will have no impact on angry feelings.
  Reasoned argument will fall on deaf ears. Let the person
  cool down first.
- *Do not allow the angry person to become a dominator.* If the
  person cannot regain control after several minutes, ask
  what would help them to cool down, or suggest they sit
  quietly for a few minutes.
- *Respect the conventions of the group.* In a structured

exercise or learning process such as action learning or a Balint group, stick firmly to the time boundary, and use the review process (which can be extended if necessary) to think together about what has happened. Make sure to consider the link between the anger and the work situation being discussed.

While all this is going on, there is some time to think. Below are some questions to consider. This is preparation for the second stage of dealing with anger, helping the group to make sense of the explosion and to use it as far as possible to contribute to achieving the task. When the group can discuss again, these and further questions can be discussed to normalize the situation and to learn from what has happened.

Allow your curiosity free rein

- How does it affect you if someone is angry with you? How does it affect you if someone is angry with someone else in your presence? Fear is a common response to anger, and can prevent us thinking. Stay aware of how you are usually affected by someone expressing anger at you, and give yourself time to think.
- Who is angry with whom? What appears to have caused it? Does everyone see it in the same way?
- What is the angry group member expressing on behalf of the group? If two people are angry at each other, what conflict are they playing out for the group?
- How comfortable is this group with conflict? Do they normally disagree robustly, politely, or not in words at all? How far outside their normal way of operating is this incident?
- How does the anger relate to the work being discussed, relationships in the team or group, and/or the broader organizational context? What information does it bring in that was not fully realized before?

When you are working with a team, the second stage of discussing an angry outburst is a particularly useful learning opportunity, since people who work together regularly have to cope with friction and mutual irritation. Understanding and learning from the anger can become a task shared between the angry person and everyone else, encouraging a reintegration of the team.

Team conflict: when it has become possible to discuss things again

- *Encourage expression of feelings.* Remember that many people fear or dislike the expression of anger. When things get calm enough for others to become involved again, encourage people to say how they felt during the angry conflict. It is important for everyone, including the protagonist(s), to say something of their own reaction to what has happened. This allows the angry person to express feelings other than anger.
- *Encourage the team to learn from the anger to improve its performance.* It is your role to help the team refocus on its task, *including* making sense of the anger and their reactions to it. Again, your curiosity is your friend. What has led up to this explosion? How does this experience affect their view of the task? What needs to be taken into account in going forward? What is the next step in going forward?
- *Encourage the team to learn about effective disagreement.* Incorporating disagreement and dealing with conflict is an essential skill for every successful team. The angry incident gives this team a chance to think about how they want to go about their disagreeing. Make full use of the opportunity. It is likely that someone will suggest agreeing some conflict 'ground rules' (better than you proposing it). What would they like to happen next time someone feels so strongly about something? What would they prefer to avoid? How can they make sure important disagreements about the work are expressed? What would help them raise and discuss differences before someone reaches boiling point?
- *Encourage the team to learn about coping with conflict.* Ground rules are useful, but not sufficient. What would each individual like their colleagues to know about how they react to anger? And about how they behave when

they feel angry? What is the best way for others to treat them when they are angry?

- *Join up thinking and feeling about the source of the conflict.* Encourage everyone to express their understanding of the angry conflict. If it is a team relatively unused to talking about feelings, consider introducing the idea of the 'process break' to give members a mechanism that validates discussing *how* they work together, reminding them that this gives very practical support to getting the job done.
- *Notice patterns in the team's dynamics.* If this kind of thing happens regularly, what does it mean? What does the individual gain by it? What does the team gain by it? What is avoided by the angry conflict?

Holding the group or team through conflict and struggle

Some groups are more difficult to hold than others, and most groups will 'have their moments'. The well-known Tuckman[153] taxonomy of a group's life 'forming, storming, norming and performing' suggests that disputes and struggles will arise once the group feels safe ('formed') enough to do so, though one should not take the idea of 'stages' of development too literally.[154] In these circumstances a steady hand and a clear voice will be important, as well as the confidence *not* to act when the group can resolve things without intervention.

> ### Some of the group coach's tools are:
>
> - willingness to acknowledge the conflict and resulting feelings
> - considering how the context of the group contributes to the conflict
> - willingness to act with authority
> - willingness to intervene if necessary
> - willingness to take the 'flak'
> - confidence to challenge unacceptable behaviour.

How best to work with a group in conflict is a question of cases, affected by factors such as the maturity of the group, the degree of organizational stability, whether it is a stranger group where everyone is equal or a team with existing power dynamics, and so on.

Vignette: Calling a spade a shovel

Misandra, the newest member of the supervision group, was presenting an in-house counselling team she had been supervising for a year and a half. Ralph and Lisa had recently left the counselling team suddenly after six and ten years respectively, and the team was reacting badly, people sniping and snapping at each other. They had agreed to spend some of their supervision time on their team dynamics.

Daniel missed the session altogether. Alan was present, even though his father had died the week before. Jessie was angry with Ralph for leaving; Liz felt that in the previous session saying 'goodbye' she was forced to be polite to Lisa, not express her true feelings; Meredith recalled her mother at her father's funeral 'presiding over a mockery'. The atmosphere was tense.

Liz spoke about not liking Lisa, and other members competed to chime in with stories of the endings of difficult relationships. During the discussion Misandra asked the group 'So it's about the necessity of hate?'

JESSIE:	Hate! That's a hard thing to say so near the end
MEREDITH:	Not a good thing to end on.
MISANDRA:	I don't see hate as the opposite of love – it's another way of being involved.
ALAN:	You mean love/hate?
MEREDITH:	I think hate is close to anger.

In the supervision group, there was a mixed response. Annabel immediately said she thought Misandra's intervention was a mistake: 'I would never use the word "hate" with clients.' The sniping of the counselling team was reproduced in the supervision group.

At the following session, the team were withdrawn, until:

PAUL: I want to challenge you about what you said about hate.

MISANDRA: Go on.

PAUL: It's a strong word to use – I don't like it.

JESSIE: Yes – it's strong.

MEREDITH: Children say it in the playground – I hate you – but they're friends the next day – it's not in the true meaning of the word.

MISANDRA: What is the true meaning?

MEREDITH: To do with anger – I don't know really – we need a dictionary.

JESSIE: Ah well – I looked it up in a dictionary actually – I was thinking quite a lot about what you said – something about what we didn't want showing us what we did.

MEREDITH: What did the dictionary say?

JESSIE: Lots of stuff – but something about things being opposed. And I realized that I hate things about my mother – how suffocating she is.

ALAN: I hate my Dad at the moment – for leaving us. I know it's not right, he couldn't choose, but . . .

MISANDRA: It doesn't change how strong the feeling is –

ALAN: That's right.

PAUL: When I used that word to Avril, it finished the relationship.

JESSIE: Maybe you need to sometimes. Human resources have been behaving much better since I had a go. Maybe you were right Paul.

It was fitting end to a conversation that had started with Paul, for the first time, challenging Misandra. There was a

> sense of relieved tension. The team, who had been stuck in mourning the loss of their colleagues, now were able to move on. Their attention moved back to their client work, and at their subsequent sessions they reported, and evidenced, better working relationships.
>
> Misandra's supervisor congratulated her on having developed a 'good feel' for what was needed by the group: it was a correct decision to allow some time to study the group dynamics, and speaking of 'the necessity of hate' had allowed the feelings underlying the covert rivalry in the team to be acknowledged and discussed. The provocation allowed Paul (on behalf of the group) to be angry with Misandra, and so for the anger to be explored.

There is a strong relationship between loss, mourning and destructive feelings. Every loss reactivates earlier losses, and can impede 'moving on'. The team members were able to express their anger, and so free themselves of the repetitive low-grade conflict through which they had been communicating it.

When someone is crying or distressed

- *Take time.* Distress will take a little time to deal with, so let go of other objectives for the moment. Offer tissues if appropriate, and allow the person to talk and calm down. In a work situation many people will be further distressed or embarrassed at showing their distress. See also the passage concerning a crying team member in 'Holding difficult feelings: using all the information about work' in Chapter 2.
- *Encourage expression in words, and acknowledge it.* Gently encourage the distressed person to put what they feel into words. Acknowledge what is said, and encourage others to express their responses. Empathy in the room will help the distressed person feel more normal again.

- *Be aware of your own feelings.* How does it make you feel to be with someone who is crying? Be aware of your own response.
- *How does the distress relate to the work?* The distress may be relevant to the work in hand, and be useful information for learning. What information does the crying carry? How could understanding it contribute to the task in hand?
- *What feeling underlies the tears?* Remember for example that some people cry when they are angry.
- *Respect the conventions of the group.* In a structured learning group, it is most likely to be the turn-taker who gets distressed, and the distress is likely to have relevance for the learning; when the worst of the distress has passed, encourage her/him to make the connections. If it is someone other than the turn-taker who gets distressed, you need to signal that the turn-taker's 'slot' will be protected, perhaps by taking 'time out'.
- *Protect the distressed person's right to their feelings.* Sometimes distress is made worse for the distressed person by others. Through the empathic sensors of our implicit knowing, the distress of others puts us in touch with our own vulnerability. Some people as a result deny or dismiss the distress of others. If this happens, comment on and discourage it.
- *Encourage the group to learn.* This is a learning opportunity for everyone on the group, to reflect on how they are affected by encountering the distress of another person. Encourage each person to reflect on their reactions and their behaviour. How do they behave when they are distressed? What would be a helpful response from colleagues?
- *Protect the goals of the group.* If the distress does not abate in several minutes, ask the person what would help them recover their capacity to continue working in the group; they may want to take a few minutes out of active work. If they can manage to stay in the room while doing so, it generally allows an easier reintegration.
- *Notice any manipulative patterns.* If someone *regularly* cries in group meetings, you may be dealing with

something quite different to ordinary distress: a bid for attention, an avoidance of a difficult discussion, or a plea for special treatment. Here your reactions and your curiosity will guide you. When does the distress arise? What feelings are evoked in other people? What does the person gain from the delay or diversion caused by the distress? What does the team gain from it? Is it always the same person – if yes, why doesn't anyone else seem to feel distress? Does the crying have any relation to demands made on the person by the group? See the vignette about manipulative crying below ('The limits of coaching').

Dealing with people who are dominating

Dealing with a dominator in a group is no time for the group coach to be a 'shrinking violet'. People who speak too much need active help, first from you and ultimately from the group, to gain a more realistic picture of their effect on others, and to modify their behaviour.

Opening gambits

- *Notice* when *and* with whom *it is happening*. Near the start of the group? In a group with strong tensions? Some people talk too much when they are anxious. Consider tactics to make the group feel safer, such as giving a stronger lead yourself.
- *Be active in challenging*. Dominating behaviour will undermine the group if you allow it to go on. You must be active in challenging it and, where it is persistent, train the group to be active in challenging it too.
- *Interrupt*. Summarizing the last point the speaker made, or building on it, and asking others to give their response.
- *Bring others in*. Asking others to give their view; invite specific individuals to speak if you have observed someone who seems to have a view.
- *Use gesture*. Put your hand up as the dominator begins, and gesture to another member to speak.
- *Restate the fundamentals*. Restate that all sides of a

question can only be explored if everyone has the opportunity to put their perspective across.

If it goes on

- *Point out the dominance and invite the group to resolve it.* With marked or persistent dominators this is your main strategy. To open the discussion, say something like 'We seem to be letting xxx do too much of the work. What do others think about . . .?'
- *Comment on the pace.* To have a fruitful discussion it is important for people to have time to think, which cannot happen if the pace is too fast and furious. Ask everyone to limit the length of their contributions. This allows you to be more direct in challenging the dominator when they transgress.
- *Try humour.* Point the behaviour out in a humorous way; be careful to challenge the *behaviour* rather than putting down the individual. Humour is less likely to be useful than an explicit approach, but it may be appropriate with some groups, particularly where there is a limited capacity or willingness to think about process. You can sometimes use humour with individuals, particularly when your other signals to speak less have been ignored.
- *In a structured learning group.* Remind everyone of the protocols, especially the primacy of the turn-taker's reflection and learning, and the need for a calm pace in order to think.
- *Be persistent.* A persistent dominator will need persistent correction. Be prepared to be the broken record. Your modelling that the dominator can be stopped will encourage other group members to do it too.

Although the first task is to shut the person up so that others can speak, this is only a stopgap. It helps the other people in the group in the short term, but does not change the underlying feeling that makes the person speak so much. They are likely to repeat the pattern. If you continue to be the only one to shut them up, the group is likely to become less free in its responses in general. The whole group needs to be involved. If they continue to leave it to you, become curious about why that is. Here are some further strategies.

- *Give feedback.* It will be necessary to draw attention to the pattern to help the dominator realize what s/he is doing, and what the effect is on the group. Dominators lack empathy and so need feedback.
- *Contrast communication and speech.* Paradoxically, sometimes people speak a lot as a way of avoiding communication. The spate of words bemuses the listeners and only confusion is conveyed. Make the confusion explicit and involve the group in becoming more thoughtful about how each of their communications contributes to the task. You can also use this to check the flow from the dominator – how does what they are saying contribute to the group's progress on the task?
- *Ask about what the others in the group get out of it.* Dominators can only dominate if the rest of the group let them. How does everyone else gain? Are they let off the hook? Are they afraid to challenge a boss or senior colleague? Are they relieved of the need to take a risk? Raising the question of what the rest of the group gains is an understated way of making the domination an explicit group problem, and involving the group in resolving it.
- *Become curious about what the dominator gets out of the domination.* Is it status? Is it reassurance? Is it attention? Is it control? Is it an avoidance of the issues? It is helpful to clarify your own ideas about the source of the over-activity. For group coaches, it is usually *not* helpful to make these ideas explicit, but an opportunity may arise to invite the dominator to reflect on their own behaviour.
- *Take the dominator aside.* The problem must be resolved in the group, but some dominators may benefit from one-to-one feedback and an opportunity to reflect – in effect individual coaching to help them work more effectively in the group.

When someone is silent or over-quiet

In any group, some members are more active than others, and engagement should not be confused with speech. The group coach aims to allow each member of a group to govern their own style of involvement at a level balancing safety and risk.

Although silent group members may benefit by witnessing and identifying with the efforts of more active members, particularly in short-term groups, they can nevertheless gain more by achieving a more active role. Research has demonstrated that the most vocal group members tend to gain most, irrespective of what they say, through a sense of involvement, the regard of others which leads to self-regard.[155] In other words, active group participation is self-rewarding. Further, the group or team is impoverished if some members are almost always quiet. Their viewpoints are simply not available.

Silence, like any other group behaviour, is a communication: it means something. People are quiet for many reasons: fear of expressing too much emotion or self-disclosure; fear of self-assertion, or provoking conflict; standards of perfection so exacting that the risk of falling short by speaking is too great; a need for distance or superiority; expressing annoyance (sulking); or, like the dominator, a bid for attention, albeit in a very different style.

The group coach needs to stay as connected as possible to the meaning of the silence, which may of course change over time, paying attention to non-verbal cues and what speech is offered.

Learning the courage to speak up in a group is an important life skill, of which the quiet member needs at least some ('Practising courage and freedom to act' in Chapter 4). The middle way is wisest in dealing with quiet members: putting them on the spot, but not too much. This can be done:

- with eye contact
- by gesture
- by inviting comment on someone else's contribution
- by question
- through a 'go round' where *everyone* must comment
- through structured exercises that demand and equalize participation.

With persistently quiet members, especially in a team, it is likely to be necessary to comment more directly on the silence and its impact, by acknowledging it ('Are you open to being prodded today?') or by inviting others to reflect on their understanding of the silence, and then referring their thoughts to the silent member for judgement. See the vignette, 'Developing courage' in Chapter 4.

When someone is playing 'yes but'

'Yes but' is a 'game people play' recognized by Eric Berne in his classic book.[156] Someone playing 'yes but' first asks the group for help by presenting a problem, but then rejects any help offered. Her/his problems are insurmountable, and every attempt to help fails. In an extreme form, the group member will be interested only in her/his own problems and will relate to the group only as the one most in need of help.

The other group members try to help for a while, then become irritated, then frustrated. The 'yes-butter' can be very subtle in their refusals of aid, sometimes rejecting help overtly, sometimes covertly, and sometimes appearing to accept while ignoring what is offered. If the behaviour is allowed to continue, it can undermine the effectiveness and cohesiveness of the group.

'Yes but' needs tackling in the same way as persistent dominator behaviour (see 'Dealing with people who are dominating' above), through identifying the pattern, and regular feedback from all members on its impact. It may also be helped by a paradoxical injunction, such as the coach agreeing with the member that it is all quite hopeless.

When someone's contribution is always boring

We are idiosyncratic in our boredoms. Still, sometimes in our work with groups we come across someone whose lack of spontaneity and risk-averseness renders their contributions quite deadening. They say what is safe and unlikely to give offence to anyone. Their self-censorship is instinctive, and their conflict-aversion extreme. They are burdened by an excess of the social sensitivity that inhibits most people some of the time.

The task of the group coach is to help the inhibited group member to reduce their editing of their responses so as to express some of their truer and more spontaneous responses. This is likely to take time. A paradoxical injunction here is likely to come off as sarcastic, and too direct an approach as intimidating. Tact is required. Sometimes light-hearted structured exercises, particularly early in the group's work, can help this individual to 'speak a true word in jest'. In general, understated questioning and encouragement to say what they really think is the way forward, together with praise when they do take a risk.

When someone cannot acknowledge anything but logic

At times in coaching groups or teams we come across individuals who seem to have a very limited emotional range, and appear unmoved by emotions in circumstances where most people would be. Since, as we have seen in Chapter 2, emotional content is a component of every interaction, such people can find themselves isolated and distant from others. They are unlikely to volunteer for coaching groups, but may be obliged to come, by managers who perceive their need for greater skill at interacting with colleagues. If so, it is helpful to discuss their motivation openly and see if logic can offer some reasons why they should try to engage.

What we are talking about here goes well beyond the brisk manner thought to demonstrate efficiency and competence in many business environments. It is a suppression of feeling so thorough that very little ever breaks through. In team coaching we meet these individuals sitting always somehow at the edge of the group, sometimes literally as well as metaphorically. They feel indifference to most ordinary events and relationships. They have often won a place by their consistency, or their capacity to apply thinking to their own range of work, but have little empathy for others, or for the broader vision. Colleagues who have at first attempted a closer connection have given up, and they are regarded with incomprehension and, at best, a kindly tolerance. In any team coaching exercise they are highly task-focused because, to them, interaction is a foreign language best left unlearned.

To integrate these people more fully is a long-term undertaking, small step by small step; the group's acceptance is an essential precondition. The 'logical' ones do not completely lack feeling. If they acknowledge some small emotion, like minor irritation or hurt, ask them to look at it through a microscope and describe it. Observe expression and other non-verbal cues carefully and ask about them. Help them to observe and comment on the reactions in their own bodies – butterflies in the tummy, clenched fist. An apparently small step here is really a giant one, so limited objectives are realistic. Perseverance is essential, and as the group coach you can model to the rest of the group or team how to help the individual gradually become more involved.

When someone is so self-centred they cannot work on the task

Such a character does not need much describing; they are so self-centred that their conversation is always about themselves. In a team they will not cooperate readily or understand the needs of others; in any group situation they are likely to be either disruptive or withdrawn. If they do participate they will monopolize the conversation and likely be critical of the undertaking if any challenge is made. They will either be overly sensitive to criticism or impervious to any criticism because of their conviction of their own specialness.

Vignette: The limits of coaching

Rebecca was the last to join the corporate events team. She professed herself a team player but in fact did far less than anyone else on the many shared tasks, though she made a point of always being visible to senior people.

Every shared task she did take on, she talked about endlessly, complaining of others' laziness. In team coaching sessions, whenever she was challenged about this, she would burst into tears as the rest of the team looked on helplessly. The coach gave her space to calm down and despite several attempts could not oblige her to engage with the feedback; Rebecca simply began to cry again. The coach acknowledged the impasse in the group, and privately advised Ginny, the manager, that Rebecca's problem went too deep for tackling through coaching.

This is an example of an inappropriate use of team coaching, on two counts. Ginny was trying to use the sessions to manage Rebecca's failures of performance, properly a one-to-one activity; and Rebecca's problem was too deep-rooted to be resolved through normal coaching.

This kind of problem is beyond the scope of coaching. Sometimes coaching can curb the self-obsessed behaviour, through feedback and through the kinds of tactic used with dominators, but the underlying problem is likely to reassert itself; it is a problem that can be managed, not solved.

In this chapter we have looked at how to deal with problematic individual behaviour in groups. In the next chapter we consider how to approach groups who do not collaborate effectively.

Groups that do not work: understanding and tackling dysfunctional patterns in group behaviour

This chapter contains:

- This chapter
- Anxiety in groups
- What if . . . there is lateness and absence?
- What if . . . a number of people look bored, restless or disengaged?
- Bion: a theory of group dysfunction
- The 'basic assumptions'
- Working with unconscious and unspoken conflicts
- Teams declared 'dysfunctional'
- The drama triangle
- Working with conflicting messages
- Argyris' theory of organizational defences
- Finally

This chapter

The previous chapter was concerned with problematic individual behaviour encountered in groups; this chapter discusses groups that do not work. It reviews the impact of anxiety on group functioning, and goes on to discuss a couple of typical problems. It introduces Bion's ideas about underlying patterns in non-functioning groups. Through extended consideration of a vignette, it looks at the dynamics of teams declared 'dysfunctional', and outlines the 'drama triangle' dynamic. It discusses unspoken conflicts, and the implications of Chris Argyris' theory of organizational defences for group coaching practice.

Anxiety in groups

Anxiety is a major reason for groups not working well. The conditions in an anxious group are precisely opposite to those in a group that is well-held: people do not feel confident to take risks, and so it is difficult to learn.

People are more likely to feel anxious in groups:

- the larger the group gets, particularly larger than ten people
- when members don't know each other well
- meeting infrequently
- with an inconsistent membership
- that have no clear structure/accepted way of doing things
- when the group cannot achieve its aims, or when there is disagreement about aims or how to achieve them
- when there is pressure from outside.

How we deal with anxiety is central to coaching a group. At the start of the life of any group, most members, and perhaps the coach, tend to be anxious: the coach must help members feel less anxious, so as to be able to work. Members need to feel that the coach is relaxed, and has clear goals and expectations about the work, and from them. (If you do not feel relaxed, at least take steps to *look* relaxed.) This leadership role can be gradually relinquished as the group settles to its task.

Even if it were possible to remove all anxiety, it would not be desirable. A degree of anxiety helps us perform, but the degree is all-important. You want group members to feel safe enough to take a risk (which temporarily increases anxiety) in the service of the task. Sometimes a group is *too* comfortable, and the coach will need to challenge complacency.

> ### What kinds of behaviour in a group suggest anxiety?
>
> * Lateness or excessive earliness
> * Talking too much
> * Withdrawn silence
> * Intellectualizing
> * Poor listening demonstrated by irrelevant or inappropriate questions or contributions
> * Inappropriate use of humour
> * Whispering to a neighbour
> * Smoothing over all difficulties
> * Continually apologizing
> * Finding fault with everything.

There are many, many kinds of behaviour in groups that indicate anxiety, often completely outside of people's awareness. The coach must be aware of the influence of anxiety, acknowledge and normalize its presence, and start work with the group anyhow. This will allow the conflicts hindering work to emerge and be examined.

What if . . . there is lateness and absence?

Warning: The remarks about punctuality may not translate to all cultures.

The prime working time of any group is when everyone is in the room together. Setting the correct tone from the start is the key factor in dealing with absences and lateness.

Stressing from the start the importance of everyone being present for the whole coaching session communicates your seriousness about the group's work, and puts a pressure on members to do likewise. Naturally, travelling and other difficulties do arise, and at times the group coach must help the group manage members' lateness. 'Business as usual' is usually the best approach, with a brief pause as the late-comer arrives. Absences are more problematic, for both the

Vignette: Setting the tone

In the first meeting of an action learning set, one of the members announced that she would have to miss the next session. It was no accident that she was the most ambivalent member of the group. The coach insisted on a protracted negotiation to find a date that would work, without success. The discussion emphasized, however, how seriously the coach took attendance. No one else missed a session, despite some serious professional and personal challenges; members always gave notice of late arrival, and rarely were more than a few minutes late.

absent member and the others. The coach must have in mind the question of the meaning of the absence, and the question of how the group reintegrates at the next session.

Norms about lateness vary. An experienced corporate coach was shocked at the 'relaxed' attitude to timekeeping she found in parts of the voluntary sector, and beat a hasty retreat! In any sector, however, it is important to make explicit the impact, at the very least in terms of working time lost, of lateness, drop-ins, early departures and so on.

Routine lateness and absence among several members is serious: members 'voting with their feet'. This is best tackled at the level of the group as a whole, by wondering about its meaning. Remember, every event in the life of a group is a communication (see 'Communication' in Chapter 3); this is a shout. There may be several reasons, either in the organizational context or in the group itself. Engage honestly with what comes up, and engage the whole group in the process of deciphering the meaning. Doing so will usually have the side-benefit of improving attendance and punctuality.

What if . . . a number of people look bored, restless or disengaged?

They probably are. Like every event in the life of the group, this is a communication. Try to understand it. Since group coaching is about making meaning more articulate, check out your perception and see what can be uncovered. Listen and watch carefully to catch the emotional tone as well as the words. It is best to take this up with the whole group rather than homing in on individuals.

Allow paranoia to be on hold, and do not assume that the responses are about you or your style; they are just as likely to be about the organization, or perhaps each other. Are you sure that these people are volunteers, or were they sent? Are the coaching goals, goals to which they are committed? Do people in the group have any previous history that needs to be understood before proceeding? Anger often underlies boredom: what might they be annoyed about? (People are often more willing to acknowledge annoyance, irritation or frustration than anger.) If they are angry about some organizational injustice, what could they do to put things right?

Address the group where they are, and go for a quick win. For instance, 'what would help this team work together a bit better?', 'how would you know if that had happened?' are more useful questions to a struggling team than 'what would it take for this team to be the best in the company?'.

If the group members were 'sent', what could they get from the experience that would be valuable to them? One coach uses the concept of 'prisoners, tourists and enthusiasts' in his workshops. He shares the idea with the group and uses it to engage individuals in monitoring their own motivation.

If people are discontented with some aspect of the coaching group, engage them in defining how to improve it – by redefining goals, roles or operating rules. If they are discontented with you, encourage them to clarify what role they want you to fulfil. Often this simple discussion will get things moving again. Agree how to review things if the problem recurs.

Bion: a theory of group dysfunction

Wilfred Bion defined three 'basic assumptions'[157] that impede a group's work, founded on his observation of groups. Bion was a visionary whose work is about deeply unconscious processes of which group members will mostly be unaware, but which can at times be observed in group behaviour. The basic assumptions are ways of group members managing repressed anxiety, a flight from reality and the difficulties of being in a group. The three basic assumptions are:

- fight/flight
- dependency
- pairing.

Anxiety, fear, hate and love are common to all three group states, but fight/flight is characterized by anger and blame, dependency by guilt and depression, and pairing by unfounded messianic hope. The root of the basic assumptions is an instinctive fear of group disintegration, perhaps surviving from a time when individual survival was only possible through group survival. All three aim to preserve the group at the expense of members' individual well-being, or the group's ability to work. They apply in groups of all sizes, but are felt more keenly in larger groups.

The 'basic assumptions'

- *Fight/flight.* A group that has gathered together for fight/flight is a united group – united against a common enemy. Its unity is emotionally satisfying. If the group has no obvious 'enemy', then the next best thing is to find a leader to whom the enemy *is* obvious; if the enemy is 'within' the group, it is scapegoating.
- *Dependency.* The assumption in a dependency group is that one person, often the group leader, will supply the needs of the group members; other members are in a position where their needs are to be supplied. There is little mutuality in the arrangement.
- *Pairing.* The group met together for the purposes of 'pairing off' provides temporary relief from the trials of the other two basic assumptions, but is no more productive.

Sometimes it is expressed through two group members engaging each other in an exclusive conversation, while others watch. Through pairing the survival of the group will be secured. There is a sense of unjustified messianic hope.

The basic assumptions are deeply unconscious; group members will not articulate them or be directly aware of them, but they will *act* as though guided by the currently dominant assumption. The coach can sometimes name the assumption so as to help the group escape its grip.

Vignette: Fight/flight

An outreach team in the Mental Health Trust was told that it had been selected for closure, its functions to be taken over by another department. The staff group of thirty met together a few days after the announcement, which had been insensitively handled. Reactions ranged from overwhelmed disbelief, to feeling that their work was neither understood nor valued by the senior Trust officials who made the decision, to concern for the patients, some of whom were severely depressed or suicidal, to considerable anger against the managers, the staff of other departments, the government, and society for not caring for its most vulnerable members. Junior staff and leaders were united in their feelings, though their analysis of the situation differed.

The group coach let the discussion run for some time. Then she commented 'You seem to be united against the common foe, which might lead to things being overlooked'. The group paused as though to digest something. In the ensuing discussion plans were made to represent the dangers of the proposal forcibly to people who might influence the outcome; one or two members aired unconnected work concerns, which had the effect of reassuring those with similar challenges, restoring 'business as usual', and helping the group recover its ability to work.

In the vignette, the 'uniting to fight' had some basis in reality. The coach's intervention about 'fight/flight' was effective in part because the discussion made the observation hard to deny. In many cases the 'uniting to fight' has little relation to reality, as with the team busy blaming some other part of the system (HR, production or HQ) for their lack of productivity. The blaming stance is a defence against thinking, often facilitated by someone's willingness to be its spokesperson.

While any of the basic assumptions dominate thinking, the group is unable to work freely and creatively, nor can members act with autonomy. Group behaviour and decisions are governed by the assumption. The assumptions are more likely to operate at times of stress. The basic assumption may shift from one to another three times within an hour, or one basic assumption may hold sway for months. A shift to a different basic assumption will create short-term relief, but the group is still avoiding work on its task.

Working with unconscious and unspoken conflicts

Groups get stuck in a non-working position because they are unconscious of the conflicts that impede them. A team can collaborate despite mutual hostility, but not when the hostility is hidden or unconscious. It will constantly disrupt the work. Similarly, positive feelings towards each other may obstruct work, through an unwillingness to upset each other by raising unpalatable facts.

Conflicts are amplified in the group through the mechanisms described in Chapter 3. The group coach is therefore in a good position to study them: a group conflict will communicate itself to the coach, often through the invitation to play a role or occupy a position rather different to what was written in the contract. The invitation will be not be communicated in words. Here are some roles for which the coach may not have intended to audition:

- cheerleader to the apathetic
- the enemy
- allied with the enemy
- behind a soundproof screen

- politely ignored
- powerless babysitter
- the fount of all knowledge
- rescuer
- persecutor
- victim.

Clients can be very resistant to noticing or acknowledging these forces. In the vignette opposite, the coach had shared his analysis of the work needed during contracting. The sponsor, the HR Director, had agreed to the dual objectives of the programme, including the priority of tackling the hostile stance of the managers. At review she disowned this view and concentrated on the subsidiary training goals. After its resolution, the very existence of the conflict was denied. See also the discussion below.

Teams declared 'dysfunctional'

When a team has been declared 'dysfunctional' or, worse, has come to adopt that view of itself, members' expectations of coaching are likely to be low. It is helpful to speak individually with all team members to gauge where the levers for change might be. Clear and rigorous goal-setting is important, but the key work will be to clarify the paradoxical or conflicting beliefs and goals as they emerge. Bear in mind that the team may well be carrying 'dysfunction' for the larger organization, and so the resistance to changing the label there, may be at least equal to the resistance in the team itself.

If the dysfunction centres on overt conflict within the group, see 'Dealing with anger in a group' in Chapter 9.

The organization in the vignette is a good example of a culture in which there is an oscillation between dependency and fight/flight basic assumptions. All the managers had an expectation that the organization would look after them, strengthened by their feelings about losing the autonomy of their small agencies. The new CEO was disliked not only as the rather controlling agent of change, but also because failures by the new organization were experienced as failures

Vignette: Management development with a 'dysfunctional' group

Jerry has been hired by the HR Director for a not-for-profit organization providing services to victims of crime. The members of the group previously ran small independent agencies, now amalgamated into one regional organization of which they are branch managers. 'Disaffected' does not adequately describe their position; they are hostile and so locked in conflict with the new regional centre that there is little communication. The CEO, the driving force behind the change, wants a management development programme to improve standards of work, and to get the branches in line with the new regional centre.

Jerry explains to the HR Director that the group will have to trust him for the process to work, and that the programme's dual objectives will require a flexible coaching approach where the needs of the participants have higher priority than the formal training targets.

At the opening event, the managers are highly critical of the CEO as 'very controlling and ambitious', and of many aspects of the new arrangements, as not supporting their services adequately. They let off a lot of steam, and by the end of the opening day express themselves ready to move on. They start the programme with enthusiasm. Jerry adopts a pragmatic coaching approach and helps them function more effectively together, both in tackling their grievances with regional office and in sharing their new learning.

He introduces the drama triangle as a way of thinking about the dynamics in the organization, with the roles of persecutor, victim and rescuer moving around between region, branches, him, the CEO and HR. He emphasizes the need to be conscious of this 'dance' in order to step out of it.

As time goes on, members become more open, and it is clear that there are very different positions in the group. Some managers are genuinely engaged and keen to sort out the problems and go forward with improved services. Some are willing to try to make things work, and test progress step by step; this is the largest group. A few are interested only in maintaining a sense of grievance, and encouraging as many others as possible to join them.

By the end, Jerry is satisfied that the group overall has made good progress. Members have pooled resources and expertise, and developed a habit of thinking together about how to tackle problems. They think more strategically about their services, and have made some progress against the training goals. The attitude of most of the group to the regional centre is now questioning, rather than irrationally hostile.

At the programme review with the HR Director, Jerry finds that her view is less positive. She seems uninterested in discussing the improvement in relationships between branch and centre that was her main goal before. She focuses instead on the training goals, in particular on the ones that she doesn't feel have been met. Jerry resists this analysis, reminding the HR Director of the goals of the programme.

of care for which she was responsible. She had united the managers to fight her, and the group Jerry encounters at first is united only by this common hatred. As the basic assumption shifts, differentiation emerges within the group and different stances can be expressed.

The drama triangle (see opposite) was a useful metaphor because the explanation freed some of the managers to achieve a more adult position, where they made their peace with the change and began to negotiate for what they needed.

By the end of the coaching, all the managers accepted the new structure as a fact, and the majority were better equipped to manage, were sharing expertise and help, and were negotiating together to get what they needed from the regional centre. The disaffection of a few managers, however, was more entrenched. They continued to blame 'regional' for all problems and refused to take responsibility for improving things. So had Jerry done a good enough job?

On the one hand, coaching cannot replace normal performance management. Peer pressure can improve performance, but the responsibility for dealing with persistent poor performance lies with the organization, not the coach. On the other hand, had the group's resistance to change 'located' itself more firmly in the individuals apt for it, through the process? The reluctant acceptance of the new status quo by most of the team was achieved in part by their sense of 'there but for the grace of God go I' as they listened (again) to their recalcitrant colleagues.

The drama triangle

Jerry used the drama triangle,[158] a conceptual tool derived from transactional analysis. The roles of the players in the drama are shown below.

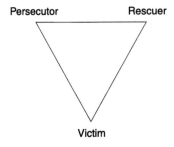

The persecutor

Sets unnecessarily strict limits	Blames
Criticizes	Keeps the victim down
Is mobilized by anger	Has a rigid, authoritarian stance
Is intimidating	Is inquisitorial

The rescuer

Rescues when doesn't really want to	Feels guilty if s/he doesn't rescue
Condescends	Keeps the victim dependent
Is self-righteous and holier-than-thou	Expects to fail and allow the victim to fail
Is well-intentioned	Loves to help

The victim

Feels helpless, hopeless, powerless	Complains
Whines	Seeks a rescuer to keep up powerlessness
Denies responsibility and blames	Depends on rescuer
Manipulates	Takes 'dejected' stance

The drama triangle still held some members of the organization in its grip. The disaffected managers persisted in seeing themselves as victims, with 'regional' as the persecutor and Jerry as an (inadequate) rescuer. The regional centre, represented by the HR Director, saw themselves as victims of this recalcitrance, again with Jerry as an inadequate rescuer. The dynamic of real (criminal) persecutors and victims in the organization's work made the dynamic particularly pernicious and entrenched.

The dynamic shifts constantly between the roles. Jerry was in danger of being 'victimized' by the HR Director for perceived failures in his work. The adult stance achieved by the majority of the group was perceived by the HR Director as a failure, because the CEO, insecure in her new role, had been unconsciously hoping for compliance – that Jerry would 'knock the managers into shape'. An unintended outcome of the coaching was that the managers as a group were more assertive in asking for the functional support that it was the regional centre's role to provide.

The regional centre was not keen to acknowledge its own weaknesses highlighted by the process, and so tried to project the failures into Jerry and his 'training'. Since she could not challenge Jerry on his coaching of the managers, the HR Director challenged him on not meeting the training goals of the programme, which had been agreed in advance to be secondary. This illustrates the resistance to change in the broader system when the 'dysfunction' shifts from the team in whom it has previously been located. The contract was only to work with the branch managers, and its success met with (perhaps predictable) resistance in the regional centre.

Jerry's robust resistance to the HR Director's characterization kept the victim role at bay, but she was unable to shift from her position, either as victim or as persecutor. If the regional centre continued to ignore its own 'dysfunctions', what Jerry had achieved with the managers would be under steady pressure. The meeting, and the contract, ended in an 'agreement to differ', and Jerry remained ambivalent about the long-term value of his work.

Working with conflicting messages

Some of the conflicts in the vignette were overt. The managers and the regional centre blamed each other for ineffectiveness, and the managers were unhappy about the loss of their small agencies' autonomy. There were further, less explicit conflicts that emerged as the work progressed, and the lack of any coaching for the regional centre presented an obstacle unresolved at the end of the assignment.

When coaching a group, the coach must win enough confidence from the group that the members are willing to engage on the explicit task; they have to feel some commitment to the goals. Jerry was candid with the managers from the outset, and encouraged them to make use of the coaching group as an opportunity for their own development, both individually and as a team.

In working with a conflicted group, it can be a good course to start work on something that relates to the explicit goals, and then await a challenge.

When the challenge comes, engage with it so as to encourage the group to express their real dilemmas. Most stuck groups are in a double bind seeking to obey conflicting messages, which keeps them stuck. Making the conflict explicit can release the knot, allowing an embracing of both sides of the paradox. Working with paradox (see 'The necessity of paradox' in Chapter 5) requires not 'choosing' one side, but keeping both sides while maintaining the tension between the two. This is an adult position and the one towards which the coach seeks to assist the group. In the vignette, two of the inconsistent messages were the managers' beliefs:

- 'regional should look after us'
- 'regional is complete crap and doesn't/can't look after us at all'.

By allowing these beliefs to be aired (explosively at first, which suggests the force with which their undiscussability had been previously maintained), Jerry helped the managers to move to a more mature position where they identified the functional support they were entitled to expect from the regional centre, and negotiated to improve it where it was inadequate.

Conflicting messages and their inconsistency must be brought into the light of day, and discussed. Thus the goals and methodology of coaching 'dysfunctional' groups and teams are the same as the goals and methodology of all group coaching: to make the communications ever more articulate (see 'Translation' in Chapter 3).

Argyris' theory of organizational defences

In Chapter 6 we examined Chris Argyris' concepts of 'espoused theory' (what I say) and 'theory-in-use' (what I do). Theories-in-use in companies have been found to be remarkably consistent around the world, encapsulated as Model I theory-in-use:[159]

1 achieve your intended purpose
2 maximize winning and minimize losing
3 suppress negative feelings
4 behave according to what you consider rational.

This theory-in-use restricts 'learning' to issues that are already discussable, so that underlying defensive routines are not threatened. Discussable problems are identified and solutions generated. These solutions may enjoy limited or initial success, but do not address the underlying problem. Those concerned now have a conflict: if they face the undiscussables, they also have to make public their previous failure or refusal to face them; Model I is then reinforced, as people deny their share of responsibility for the failure.

Argyris has elaborated his theory of 'organizational defence routines' to explain how members of an organization reconcile conflicting views and keep themselves stuck.[160] He encapsulates it in four 'rules':[161]

• design a message that is inconsistent
• act as if the message is not inconsistent
• make the inconsistency in the message and the act that there is no inconsistency undiscussable
• make the undiscussability of the undiscussable also undiscussable.

The defence routines are therefore also undiscussable. Argyris has further elaborated the ways in which inexpert attempts to modify the theory-in-use can actually lead to its reinforcement, and the development of even more sophisticated defences against learning. 'The freedom to question and to confront is crucial, but it is inadequate. To overcome skilled incompetence people have to learn new skills, to ask the question behind the questions.'[162]

Argyris wryly comments on the wide adoption of his idea 'double-loop learning', often 'without serious attention to the behavioural conditions for its achievement'.[163] Double-loop or deutero-learning,[164] making changes both to performance (single-loop) and to the criteria by which performance is measured (double-loop), can only be sustained by an ongoing commitment and capacity in the organization to engage in rigorous *enquiry*, always seeking to reduce the undiscussable areas. This also requires commitment to rigorous enquiry from coaches, even when they fear it may lose them their clients.

Facilitation alone cannot resolve undiscussability. A facilitator may help by highlighting inconsistencies, naming 'upsetting' messages and clarifying dilemmas. This is however a short-term fix, and the group will revert to old habits as soon as the facilitator is gone. Espoused theories can easily change, theories-in-use more slowly. Team members themselves must learn to recognize and tackle the paradoxical messages that bind them, and develop their capacity to raise and discuss the previously undiscussable. The coach can make several contributions to the development of these skills in the client team.[165]

Surfacing the undiscussables

- Encourage the team to examine inconsistencies and gaps in their reasoning
- If they deny the inconsistencies, surface and make explicit the 'theories-in-use' that can be deduced from their actions
- View bewilderment and frustration as further communications concerning learning[166]
- Create opportunities for the group to practise Model II (valid information, informed choice and responsibility for implementation) enquiry methods to reduce defensive manoeuvres.

Model II theory-in-use requires team members to question the obvious and the taken-for-granted, and to take personal responsibility for their part in maintaining organizational defences. They must seek new learning as actively as reassurance. Skilled holding by the coach (see 'Holding' in Chapter 2) will ease this process.

So how difficult is it to change theory-in-use? The skills are not acquired quickly, but can be acquired through practice, given the will to do so. Argyris comments that 'most people require as much practice as is required to play a not-so-decent game of tennis'.[167] Medium- to long-term group or team coaching can leave the group in a position where their communication is more robust, and where they need the coach only for 'refreshing' or tackling problems of new depth or intensity.

How can a coach avoid bolstering Model I thinking while seeking to change it? There are no guarantees of success in this field, but skilled and psychologically informed supervision offers the coach a sustained and sustaining space in which to examine her/his own 'theory-in-use'. Better yet, a supervision group could help fuller understanding of team and organizational patterns. Success depends in large measure on the impetus for change in the team and in the broader system, as Jerry in the vignette discovered the hard way. A key factor is how defensive the client is. The wise coach looks carefully, and tests her/his diagnosis with the client, before leaping in.

Finally

Dysfunction in a team must always be understood as an expression of dysfunction in the team's broader organizational context. Accepting the label 'dysfunctional' is a risky business for the coach, as the dysfunction may not all be where it is currently 'located'. All group and team coaching contains difficulties, and difficulty is a matter of degree. Changing thinking and behaviour takes time, but understanding the psychological and interpersonal processes in Chapters 2 to 4 can help us be aware of the unspoken conflicts and defensive routines we must surface. With practice we can become more expert and courageous at helping teams disentangle their difficulties. Our chances of success are highest where conditions in the team and in the broader system support change.

Working with difficult groups and teams

- Use supervision or consultation to develop and maintain understanding
- Understand the broader forces
- Educate the client about the implications for the broader system
- Be rigorous about making the client clarify goals
- Start work on explicit goals
- Highlight paradoxes
- Be prepared for challenges
- Use paradoxes and challenges to surface the group's dilemmas
- Be prepared to tolerate discomfort
- Be rigorous in surfacing the dynamics, incongruities and gaps
- Be prepared to intervene to restore thought if the work of the group is threatened
- Attend to developing group members' capacity to express the undiscussables.

In the next chapter we examine how managing the beginnings, middles and endings of group coaching interventions can improve the chances of a good outcome.

Managing beginnings, middles and endings: boundaries of the group

This chapter

This final chapter is concerned with managing the boundaries of group coaching interventions to maximize the chances of a good outcome. It focuses particularly on the time boundaries, and the physical environment.

Coaching groups have a beginning, a middle and an end. How we manage the beginnings is critical to the group's degree of mutual trust and therefore to members' ability to learn from each other. An important part of getting the beginning right is attending to the environmental and structural factors that can contribute to learning – the 'system administration'. How we handle the middle affects how well the group works to achieve its desired outcomes,

This chapter contains:
- This chapter
- System administration: getting the conditions right
- Time and the group
- The physical environment of the group
- Other system administration issues
- Beginnings, middles and endings of group sessions: tasks and indicators
- Beginnings, middles and endings of sessions: good behaviour
- The beginning of the coaching assignment
- Setting a new group up right – the first meeting
- The middle of the coaching assignment and the transfer of learning
- Transfer of learning and good intentions
- Kolb and learning
- The ending of a coaching group
- Psychological dimensions of endings
- Unconscious feelings about endings
- Dealing with early departers
- In the final session
- Finally

and contributes to members' applying what they have learned in their normal work setting. How we manage the endings makes a difference to how members handle other work endings, and to how they remember this group.

System administration: getting the conditions right

It is not the group coach's job to get the job of the group done; group members are responsible for that.[168] The group coach's responsibility is to ensure that the conditions are as favourable as possible to work. This 'system administration', attending to the total environment of the group, includes the impact of time on the group, the physical setting, membership of the group, and liaison with the organization.

Time and the group

Time, and the consciousness of time, is an important area of coach skill. In a coaching group, the coach is holding the tension between helping the group work at a pace conducive to thinking (that is, an unhurried pace) and the consistent awareness of the time limits on the work – its beginning, middle and end. The group coach must balance working with both kinds of consciousness of time. Managing time for the group is an important part of the coach's system administration role.

Always finish on time. Members then know they can rely on it. At a non-conscious level, this reinforces group members' awareness of the real time limits on the work, helping them to stay focused and motivated.

Always start on time. If there are not enough people in the room to start on the main task, say so and make a start on something – usually possible with a little ingenuity – that can be done by a few people. With a new group, it is a good idea to have such a task in mind, in case you need it. If you choose to delay starting by a few minutes, be explicit with the group about it, so that those present know that you have noticed and that you are respectful of the time they have set aside.

Good group settings have never been more important than now, when many people work in organizations where it is almost impossible to get everyone together to work on a task, where it is commonplace for meetings to be interrupted by phone calls, members working online while in the meeting, and members arriving late or leaving early. The impact of these disruptions on work is routinely underestimated. Core working time for a coaching group is when everyone is in the room together, fully attending to the task.

A coaching group will be less effective if we accept these working conditions as normal or inevitable. An important part of the group coach's role is to stand up for the importance of uninterrupted time for the group's work, and the need for everyone to start and finish together. S/he must negotiate to secure the best possible agreements for work to take place. The time pressure is also on the coach: if late arrivals, early departures and interruptions reduce a coaching session from three hours to one and a half, s/he will find it much harder to achieve the coaching outcomes. If shifts in the pace of working life have indeed changed the bigger picture irrevocably, it is all the more important to be aware of their impact, and to protect the working space of the group.

The physical environment of the group

It is important to get the setting right to be conducive to work. The physical environment has an impact on the effectiveness of the group; a good environment – consistent, quiet, comfortable, well-equipped – will add value to an effective group, though by itself it will not make an ineffective group work. As a group coach, be particular about where your group is to work, and secure the best possible working environment for it.

The checklist overleaf shows several aspects of setting to consider. Not all will be relevant to all circumstances, but the checklist offers a 'gold standard'.

Physical environment

The group's meeting place

- Is it always the same room? This will contribute to a sense of consistency and continuity
- What is the general character and ambience of the room?
- Is the lighting adequate and pleasant?
- Does the organization or building in which the group meets ever create or allow intrusions?
- Is it the normal workplace of group members? If so, is the group's uninterrupted working time respected?

Chairs

- Are all the chairs the same? The ideal answer is 'yes'
- Is there the correct number of chairs for the group?
- Does anyone always sit in the same place?
- Where do you like to sit?
- Where do group members like to sit?
- What happens when someone is absent – does the group sit with an empty chair? How does this help or hinder the group in making sense of an absence?

Physical focus

- Is there a table and is it the right size and appropriate for the work of this group? A board-style table does not help a group trying to remove barriers to communication
- If there is no board-style table, is there a small table or other point of focus in the centre of the group?

Other system administration issues

Ground rules

- How are group ground rules arrived at?
- If you are using a particular method, such as action learning, how are its protocols refreshed?

Messages

- How are messages to the group communicated?
- How is their impact managed? As the group coach it is your responsibility to manage this for the group.

Time boundaries

- Are the start and finish time boundaries of the group understood to be binding on everyone?
- How are any variations handled?

Contact outside sessions (learning groups only)

- Is there any contact between members between group sessions?
- Is there any contact between the coach and any member between group sessions?
- If there is contact, how is the impact of the contact on the group thought about?

Beginnings, middles and endings of group sessions: tasks and indicators

Stage	Beginning	Middle	End
Tasks	Arrive, be welcomed, settle down, get basic information	Start work, share ideas, discuss context, issues, approaches and solutions, sometimes make decisions	Summarize decisions and next steps, tie up loose ends, evaluate and celebrate, say goodbye
Problems if too long	Over-cosy, frustrated, feel discussion is unreal	Getting nowhere, locked in conflict, overwhelmed, frustrated, attacked	'Already gone', time wasted, bored
Problems if too short	Anxious, uninvolved	Frustrated, unable to get a word in, uninvolved, cheated of a full discussion	Things too neatly wrapped up, solution doesn't cope with problem

Beginnings, middles and endings of sessions: good behaviour

At each stage of the group there are specific behaviours that the group coach is keen to encourage in group members. Especially at first, s/he may need to do so by example. Not all these will apply to every situation.

Activities that help at the beginning

- Welcoming people
- Raising issues
- Suggesting ways of tackling a problem
- Asking for and/or giving information
- Listening carefully
- Noticing who wants to speak/encouraging others to speak.

Activities that help in the middle

- Offering ideas/views/opinions
- Asking questions
- Differentiating information from opinion
- Acknowledging contributions
- Suggesting structures for discussion
- Clarifying your ideas or other people's ideas
- Building on your ideas or other people's ideas
- Confronting differences
- Seeking others' views and feelings
- Enthusing others
- Seeking consensus.

Activities that help at the end

- Evaluating ideas
- Summarizing arguments and facts
- Formulating proposals
- Acknowledging what has been done, and what remains to do
- A definite ending.

The beginning of the coaching assignment

What the coach does at the outset of a group coaching assignment is critical; s/he has to set the tone that is going to be most productive for this group, promoting a learning culture safe enough for people to take risks, taking account of the task, the organization's habits and culture, the individuals involved, and the relationships between them outside the group. See also 'Holding a group' in Chapter 2 and 'Anxiety in groups' in Chapter 10.

Here is a checklist for a coaching group's first meeting.

Setting a new group up right – the first meeting

- *Your* core objective is to ensure that everyone wants to come back next time
- Welcoming
- Explaining the group's objective and the process
- Consult them about what working agreements would help them work well together
- Acknowledging feelings, especially anxiety – do not say that you feel anxious, but acknowledge that it is 'normal' for 'everyone' at the outset
- Modelling – for instance, showing interest in others and their views
- Be explicit about what you want from them – for instance, that you want everyone to make a contribution and hear their own voice in the group
- Reinforcing members' positive behaviours
- Being observant of individuals
- Encouraging everyone to speak
- Keeping boundaries firm – use of agreed protocols
- Keeping boundaries firm – start and end on time.

The middle of the coaching assignment and the transfer of learning

Coaching assignments have time limits. Time limits are useful in focusing and refocusing the group on the task, and encouraging the transfer of learning to normal working life. The core skill is to hold the end in mind from the beginning, including having always a sense of where the group is in the process. Be explicit with the group about this at times: 'we have four more sessions to sort that out'. Encourage individuals and teams to break their goals down into smaller steps and review how they are doing towards achieving their main goals.

It is helpful always to 'bookmark' the midpoint of the assignment. It helps people notice that they are now in the second half of the work, and stimulates thought about the end, and what they are taking forward from the process.

As the middle becomes the late middle, you can raise the question, 'how will you keep this up after the coaching group has ended?'.

There is a line to be walked here requiring subtlety and skill. It is also an important part of the coach's role to protect unhurried time for thought, for the work to be done. The skilled coach can balance this paradox of unhurried time versus limited time through pace shifts in different parts of the session. There is also a pace to change to be respected. New insights take time to digest. Don't rush too quickly to 'how will you put that into practice?' or you run the risk of the idea not being fully grappled with, and the action being inadequately thought through.[169]

The transfer of learning is achieved in the middle of the group, not the end; it is in how the learning has been internalized. The process of summing this up at the end is a reinforcement of work that has already taken place, or it is meaningless.

Transfer of learning and good intentions

The question of how to ensure that things that we have learned stay learned is a perennial and familiar challenge for coaches and allied professionals. We know from our own experience that truths self-evident in the clear light of the coaching session can evaporate on return to normal work routine; shifts in behaviour celebrated in the group will certainly be under threat when the individual is under pressure, since we all regress to primitive ways of relating when we are under stress.

Good resolutions get broken sooner or later. Paradoxically, if the coach can help the team have tolerance of some failure in changing behaviour, it is easier for people to return to the new behaviour. The team coaching in the example 'holds' the issue of how people behave to each other through the change period. In this way failures can be understood and overcome, and improvements reinforced, over time becoming 'normal' or habitual. If it had ceased after the creation of a list of desired behaviours, this would not have happened.

242   PART 5

Vignette: Planning for failure

Mary coached the team through a difficult negotiation about how they could improve collaboration, requiring changes in behaviour from everyone. By the third session everyone had clarified what others expected from them and what they wanted from each of the others.

MARY: So you have agreed your team ground rules. What will happen when someone breaks one of them?

FRED: What do you mean? We don't intend to break them.

SHAZIA: We don't *intend* to ... but we need to know what the sanctions are when someone does.

MARY: Well, I wasn't thinking so much of sanctions as how to get things back on track.

TOM: We could talk it over at once.

KERRY: That would be best –

TOM: ... or if there wasn't time, just 'bookmark' it to discuss at our next coaching session – like we have done so far.

When they returned, George said 'It was a good thing we talked about what to do when we didn't stick to the new rules. I felt dreadful when I snarled at Kerry *and* Fred, but as it was I didn't despair, I just picked myself up, tried to do better, and I knew we could talk it through here.'

Kolb and learning

Kolb's well-known learning cycle[170] in its original form offers a simple model for thinking about the transfer of learning of group members. The cycle is continuous, and learning begins at any entry point. We can use the model in a formal way, or informally as an internal checklist.

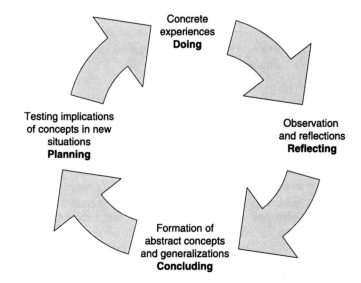

Optimal learning involves using all elements of the cycle, so it can be used to ensure that individual and group learning is thorough, engaging fully with each perspective. It is also useful in gauging individual learning styles, to tailor how to work with individuals to take advantage of their preferences, and challenge them to use their least pre-ferred ways of learning.

The ending of a coaching group

If the beginning of a group is a defining moment, the ending is also very important, but in a much less conscious way. Endings are one of the most common areas where personal feelings can undermine the work. Most of this section is concerned not with celebration but with loss and the deficit side of endings, because that is where the pitfalls lie for the coach in 'holding' the group steady.

Ending on time is crucial, in each session of the coach-ing assignment and as regards the assignment as a whole. Firm time boundaries evoke the 'holding' that makes the group feel safer, and makes challenging interactions more tolerable.

If a group coaching assignment is extended, it should be through an explicit and relatively formal discussion involving the group in reviewing its goals and timeframe together, before it is confirmed.

Psychological dimensions of endings

A prerequisite for working effectively with group coaching endings is for the coach to be aware of her/his own feelings about them. Endings are often difficult. If something is good, why would we want it to end? Or was it so challenging that our most positive feeling is relief at its conclusion? While most people can respond to the idea of a new beginning, for many of us endings are problematic, at a non-rational level.

This is to do with the way our brains work. We automatically link all new experiences (such as the end of a learning group or team coaching assignment) to previous experiences that have similar components. There is an association in our minds between this ending and all the other endings we have ever experienced. By the middle of life this will for most of us have included some painful losses such as bereavement, divorce, redundancy and so on. There is therefore an association between endings and pain. Some people will go to great lengths to avoid pain, and therefore habitually avoid endings. We all know people who 'don't do goodbyes'.

Involvement in a good coaching group is demanding, and as it comes to an end, some people who are still physically present will withdraw and begin to focus their attention on 'what's next' – they are 'already gone'. It is a bigger problem in learning groups than in intact teams since the teams will usually be going on – it is only your involvement as their coach that is coming to an end. Conversely, in a learning group, you have greater influence over how the ending will be managed.

For a team, it is important for them to notice what they are losing with your departure, and what they are gaining. What has your work meant for them? What have you represented (at a psychological level)? Have you become in some sense a part of the team, so that it is a loss to which they now need to adjust? What are your own feelings at the end of this assignment – what are you losing?

You should not be surprised at people discovering an urgent conflicting appointment so that they need to miss the final session, or leave it early, even if the coaching group has been the most positive of experiences. Some people will go further and simply not turn up. This is the most damaging response, for these individuals and for the group as a whole. The section 'dealing with early departers' below addresses this.

Unconscious feelings about endings

The difficulty in working with endings as a coach is that most of these feelings about endings are unwanted, non-rational, and not very conscious. Members may therefore not be very receptive to thinking about them. Indeed, probably at least a percentage of coaches reading this are thinking 'what is she on about?'. If these are your honest feelings, you are unlikely to work with endings at this level. Instead, stick with what you know. Do make a point of marking endings definitely, and allow people to reflect together as they say goodbye.

So, why try to help coaching group members towards a more conscious way of dealing with endings? After all, we are not working as therapists. Well, for one thing, modern organizational life requires an unprecedented volume of endings and new starts. People manage this in various ways, perhaps most commonly by 'getting on with it'.

But to begin something new in a clean way, we need to have finished with what came before, or it will continue to preoccupy us and perhaps colour our judgement in the new role. 'When I was at xxxx we did it like this' can only persist for so long. The ending also has an impact on how the group experience is remembered and subsequently metabolized. Therefore to reinforce more conscious, mature and positive styles of ending is of great value at work, promoting better performance. We can however only do this if we are ourselves conscious of the personal impact of endings.

Your core aim at the end of a group coaching assignment is to encourage members to express as honestly as possible how they feel about the ending, both positive and negative feelings. This takes us back to 'holding'. You cannot take away difficult feelings, but you can make having and expressing those feelings OK.

Most people, including coaches, have at best ambivalent feelings about endings. It is helpful to the coach to accept that her/his success rate at helping people manage mature endings is likely to be lower than in general.

Dealing with early departers

It is important at a non-conscious level that the members end together, as well as the more obvious need for having all their voices in celebrating and reviewing the learning. Coaching groups can achieve a depth and range of communication unusual in organizational life, and usually are experienced by members as important in their development.

The non-conscious impact of early departures from final sessions is therefore significant for those who remain. The departure may be experienced as dismissive, rejecting, or disrespectful, even though the early leaver intends none of this. S/he is simply leaving the difficult business of ending to everyone else. Other members may well respond 'politely' rather than honestly, even if they are conscious of these feelings. Perhaps negative feelings about someone leaving early go back to archaic times, when every member of a group was needed to bolster the chances of survival.

Resist members' impulses to leave early, and insist on the importance of completing the work together. You will not always succeed, since some people will simply present you with a *fait accompli* or have a genuinely difficult dilemma. You will succeed more often, however, if you help the dilemma to be expressed and worked on in the group.

Even more than for the group, it is important for the person who wishes to leave early to think through the meaning and impact of their wish, and perhaps to overcome it and stay. Is this a regular pattern of behaviour for them? What is gained by it? What do they think they lose? What do they think others lose? What would happen if they were to take the risk of changing the pattern and seeing something through to the end?

It is easier to deal with people who let you know beforehand that they want to miss or to leave early on the final day; it allows time to think about and discuss how to handle things.

At times someone will choose to prioritize something over the group and you, and everyone else, will see the force of their argument. This actually compounds the group's difficulties, since the more negative feelings will then be harder to express. It is your role to take these feelings seriously and encourage the group to voice them. It may help to transpose the question to an ordinary working situation such as the loss of a team member. What feelings do people have in that situation?

Always expect the group member to convince *you* that the need for early departure is genuine, particularly for the last session. Skilled avoiders of endings will have some very good reasons why it is imperative. Although it runs against ordinary politeness, maintain an agnostic posture towards these.

If you cannot persuade the early departer to stay the course, the group will not end together, and you must help the group manage that. How can the others say goodbye to the early leaver? How will s/he say goodbye? How can the impact of the departure be aired?

In the final session

The aim of the final session is for everyone to sum up their learning, clarify what they have gained and what they still need to learn, and to say goodbye. The focus of the last session should be a detailed review of individual gains and losses and of the development of the group.

For a team, the goodbyes may only be to you, the coach. For a learning group, everyone is saying goodbye to everyone else. When people have had important learning experiences together, the loss can be felt deeply.

Some questions to ask in ending a coaching group

- What has this group been like – its strengths and weaknesses?
- What have I liked or disliked about it?
- What has helped me?
- What have I (the coach) represented for you?
- What have the individuals represented for each other?
- What have individuals gained?
- How can they take forward what they have gained?
- What did they hope for?
- Did they get it?
- If yes, how could they go on getting it/ keep it?
- If no, was it realistic? Where else could it be sought?

At the end, people may need to express sad feelings at the loss of the group, or relief that it is over; reminisce about the group's successes, or say how they have felt about each other or helped each other. If needed, it is easy to devise simple exercises for marking endings. The box shows a few.

Ending rituals for coaching groups

- Saying what has been most important to us about the group
- Saying 'one thing I did and one thing I didn't get'
- Naming one positive change in how we act at work as a result of the group
- Naming one thing we are taking forward from the group in our work
- Saying one thing the person to my left has contributed to my understanding
- Saying one thing I have appreciated about that person

- Cloaks – each person wears a flipchart on their back, and everyone else writes one true, positive thing on it (water-based pens only!)
- Form a circle to pat each other on the back.
- Group make a picture poster showing what it has achieved (one flipchart and lots of pens) – no words allowed on it.

If you do propose an ending exercise, it should be consonant with the group. Coaching uses words a lot, and so most of the exercises in the box are verbal. If however you have used other methods, continue that way. Remember too that what is communicated non-verbally in the last session is at least as important as what is communicated in words. It is important that everyone participate, so choose an exercise that will not exclude. For example, touch is problematic for some people, so if you are not sure it's OK, don't. Even the 'collective pat on the back' in the box, as apparently unthreatening as a touch exercise can get, may be difficult for some.

Finally

End on time. Attending carefully to the time boundaries of our groups helps provide members with a secure base for productive work.

Afterword

Writing a book compels the writer to learn. I set out to write a book that would share some new understandings of group and team life in organizations. In the process I have been helped by many, many people and have learned a great deal from the dialogue with colleagues about the material, and about the questions. If the book encourages group and team coaches to question and reflect more on what they find in their work, it will have achieved its purpose. I commend it to my colleagues for use, discussion and as a basis for our shared and continuing learning about the secret life of groups.

Part 6

Suggested further reading

This is an eclectic list across many fields, balancing classic texts with new material. The chapter references and bibliography offer further reading leads.

Argyris, C., 1990, *Overcoming organizational defences: facilitating organizational learning*, Boston, Allyn & Bacon

Behr, H. & Hearst, L., 2005, *Group analytic psychotherapy, a meeting of minds*, London, Whurr

Berne, E., 1961, *Games people play*, London, Penguin

Brown, D. & Zinkin, L., 1994, *The psyche and the social world*, London, Routledge

Brunning, H., ed., 2006, *Executive coaching, a systems–psychodynamic perspective*, London, Karnac

Campbell, D. & Huffington, C., eds., 2008, *Organizations Connected: a handbook of systemic consultation*, London, Karnac

Capra, F., 1982, *The turning point: science, society and the rising culture*, London, Fontana

Clutterbuck, D., 2006, *Coaching the team at work*, London, Nicholas Brealey

de Maré, P., Piper, R. & Thompson, S., 1991, *Koinonia: from hate, through dialogue, to culture in the large group*, London, Karnac

Foulkes, S.H., 1990, *Selected papers of S H Foulkes: psychoanalysis and group analysis*, London, Karnac

Group Analysis, Vol. 40, No. 2, June 2006, Special edition: Supervision, London, Sage

Goleman, D., 2007, *Social Intelligence*, London, Arrow

Gutmann, D., 2003, *Psychoanalysis and management: the transformation*, London, Karnac

Handy, C., 1985, *Understanding organizations*, London, Penguin

Kets de Vries, M.F.R., 1980, *Organizational paradoxes: clinical approaches to management*, London, Tavistock

Leimon, A., Moscovici, F. & McMahon, G., 2005, *Essential business coaching*, London, Routledge

Lyth, I.M., 1969, *Containing anxiety in institutions*, London, Free Association

Miller, E., 1993, *From dependency to autonomy: studies in organization and change*, London, Free Association

Morgan, G., 1996, *Images of organizations*, London, Sage

Passmore, J., ed., 2009, *Diversity in coaching, working with gender, culture, race & age*, London, Kogan Page

Reason, P. & Bradbury, H., eds, 2008, *The SAGE handbook of action research: participative inquiry and practice*, London, Sage

Revans, R., 1982, *The origins and growth of action learning*, London, Chartwell-Bratt

Schön, D.A., 1983, *The reflective practitioner: how professionals think in action*, New York, Basic Books

Sharpe, M., 1995, *The third eye: supervision of analytic groups*, London, Routledge

Stern, D.N., 2004, *The present moment in psychotherapy and everyday life*, New York, Norton

Surowiecki, J., 2005, *The wisdom of crowds*, London, Abacus

Weinstein, K., 1999, *Action learning: a practical guide*, 2nd edition, London, Gower

Willson, R. & Branch, R., 2006, *Cognitive Behavioural Therapy for Dummies*, Chichester, John Wiley

Winnicott, D.W., 1961, *Playing and reality*, London, Routledge

Continuous professional development in the unconscious dynamics of groups and organizations

There are many providers of group training. This short list focuses on agencies working particularly with unconscious aspects of group interaction in organizational contexts.

Bayswater Institute

The Bayswater Institute brings concepts, methods and findings from the social sciences to bear on the development of organizations. It runs the annual five-day Bayswater Working Conference, based on the 'double task': members bring issues to work on in groups, and at the same time review how the group is working. In smaller groups they practise consultation. It also offers training in socio-technical systems design and action research. www.bayswaterinst.org

Group-Analytic Society (London)

Founded in 1952 by Foulkes and his colleagues, GAS promotes the development and study of group analysis (see 'Group analysis: the fundamental dynamics of group life' in Chapter 1, and Chapter 3) in all fields, including psychology, sociology, medicine, nursing, social work, counselling, education, industry, architecture, anthropology and theology. It runs regular symposia, conferences and seminars, and publishes the learned journal *Group Analysis*. Information at www.groupanalyticsociety.co.uk

Institute of Group Analysis

Also founded by Foulkes, the Institute of Group Analysis (IGA) is the UK training body for group analysis (see citations in previous entry). The IGA's focus is therapeutic, but its introductory courses offer the opportunity to explore in depth the principles of group life described in this book. There are also regular short workshops and conferences on social and organizational themes.

The IGA offers one-year introductory courses run in eleven locations: Belfast, Brighton, Bristol, Cambridge, Exeter, Glasgow, Manchester, Oxford, Sunderland, Turvey (near Bedford) and York. Go to www.groupanalysis.org and follow the local links for more information.

The IGA offers qualifying training as a group analyst in four locations: London, Bedfordshire, Manchester and Glasgow. There are also intermediate courses, combining seminars, work discussion and small group experiences applying group analytic ideas to clinical, organizational and social problems.

- For London events and courses, visit www.group analysis.org
- For Manchester events and courses, visit www.group analysisnorth.com
- For Glasgow events and courses, visit www.igascotland. org
- For Bedfordshire courses, visit www.turveygroupwork. co.uk

OPUS

OPUS is a UK-based international organization devoted to a systems psychodynamic approach to organizational life. It publishes *Organizational and Social Dynamics* and runs conferences providing learning on group relations themes. Unique to OPUS are 'listening posts' around the world, bringing together people who seek to understand national and global dynamics. More information at www.opus.org.uk

Tavistock Institute

The Tavistock Institute of Human Relations undertakes consultancy, research and professional development, and publishes *Human Relations*. The two-week annual Leicester conference is an opportunity to study group relations through experience. There is a coaching training which includes attention to psychodynamic, cultural and organizational theories and shorter professional development activities. See www.tavinstitute.org and a resource site at www.grouprelations.com

Thornton Consulting

The author's consultancy, offering workshops, professional development groups, and group or individual supervision. www.thorntonconsulting.org

Frequently asked questions

With thanks to the Association for Coaching members who asked the questions.

Question	Chapter
What techniques work best with time-poor, disengaged group members?	10
Where is the boundary between coaching a group of individuals and coaching a team?	1
How do I explore my feelings about what is happening in a group without losing sight of the goal?	2, 4, 9, 10
What do we mean by team coaching versus individual coaching of team members?	1, 7
How do I understand and make use of 'what lies beneath' the surface of the team?	2, 3, 4, 6, 10
What are the best ways to work with larger groups?	5
How is it best to work with very competitive groups?	4, 9
What do you do when one or more group members haven't volunteered to be there?	9, 10
How to handle different objectives, i.e. when team members have different personal objectives from each other, the sponsor, their managers and the overall team or group purpose?	6, 10
How to set realistic expectations when so many businesses have a short-term outlook and coaching is a long-term approach, e.g. timeframes, ongoing good practices afterwards, individual work between coaching sessions?	6

Question	Chapter
Is supervision better one to one or in groups?	8
How to reassure, build trust and create a safe space for sharing risky ideas, personal thoughts, past mistakes, etc.?	2, 4, 9, 11
How to promote cooperation and tolerance for team-working, particularly if the group is nervous, defensive, ill at ease, competitive, etc.?	9, 10
What is action learning?	7
How to encourage weaker/shyer group members to participate and have a voice?	9
How to deal with psychological issues such as transference in the interaction between group members, and between the facilitator and group members?	2, 3, 4, 6, 10
How to end the coaching intervention, and next steps for taking the learning forward?	6, 11
What to do when one member of the team is seen as the cause of all the team's problems (and sometimes is!!)?	3, 4, 9, 10
What to do when HR will not take the difficult decision (i.e. firing or moving team members to other departments) and hopes that team coaching will provide a sticking plaster for the team?	9
I'd like some good tips about setting the right scene and mood?	2, 4, 11
What to do when the sponsor is unrealistic about the timescales that team coaching can take?	6
What to do when team members find it hard to look at their own contribution to the situation and want only to blame everyone else or the organization?	3, 10
How to support the leader (or other team members) when they are under fire from the rest of the group (scapegoating)?	4
How to set up a team coaching intervention?	6
How to set up a supervision group?	8
What about telephone groups?	7
What about web-based groups?	6
What the hell is going on in that organization?	5, 10

References and bibliography

Preface

1 Kotter, J.P., 1996, *Leading change*, Boston, Harvard Business Press; Aitken, C. & Keller, S., 2009, The irrational side of change management, *The McKinsey Quarterly*, April.

Chapter 1: Introduction: what is group coaching?

2 Leal, M.R.M., 1982, Resistances and the group analytic process, *Group Analysis*, *15* (2), 97–110.

3 Goleman, D., 2006, *Social intelligence: the new science of human relationships*, New York, Random House.

4 Nicholas, J. & Twaddell, K., 2008, *Group executive coaching: 2008 global survey*, Singapore, The AIR Institute, p. 11.

5 Ibid. In this survey there was a third category of groups (still 'learning groups' in our definition), consisting of people drawn from the same organization but not the same team.

6 Up to a group-functional maximum number of people; see 'What is group coaching?' in Chapter 1.

7 Nicholas & Twaddell, op. cit., pp. 14–15.

8 Ibid., pp. 16–17.

9 Lewin, K., 1952, *Field theory in social science*, London, Harper, p. 169.

10 Nicholas & Twaddell, op. cit., p. 5.

11 Though of course other kinds of learning may happen in them.

12 Except teams of two people, which are pairs, a special type of group with different dynamics.

13 Though sometimes developing member skills to enable eventual self-facilitation is built into the contract.

14 Thornton, C., 2004, Borrowing my self: an exploration of exchange as a group-specific therapeutic factor, *Group*

Analysis, 37 (2), 305–320; available as a free download at www.thorntonconsulting.org

15   Argyris, C. & Schon, D.A., 1996, *Organizational learning II: theory, method & practice*, Reading, MA, Addison-Wesley, p. 244.

16   Foulkes, S.H., 1975, Problems of the large group from a group-analytic point of view, in Kreeger, L., ed., *The large group*, London, Karnac, p. 34.

17   Capra, F., 1982, *The turning point: science, society and the rising culture*, New York, Simon & Schuster.

Chapter 2: Learning, holding and exchange

18   Leal, op cit.

19   Whitehead, C., 2001, Social mirrors and shared experiential worlds, *Journal of Consciousness Studies, 8* (4), 12–32. He comments: ' "theory of mind" and child development research strongly support the earlier views of Dilthey (1883–1911), Baldwin (1984), Cooley (1902), and Mead (1934) that reflective consciousness depends on a shared experiential world' (pp. 30–31).

20   Goleman, op. cit.

21   Stern, D.N., 2004, *The present moment in psychotherapy and everyday life*, New York, Karnac, p. 76. Stern's distinction between non-conscious (implicitly known but non-articulated) knowledge and unconscious (repressed) knowledge is also useful.

22   Bateson, G., 2000, *Steps to an ecology of mind*, Chicago, Chicago University Press.

23   Winnicott, D.W., 1971, *Playing and reality*, London, Penguin.

24   Winnicott, D.W., 1965, The capacity to be alone, in *The maturational processes and the facilitating environment*, New York, International Universities Press, pp. 30, 45.

25   Bion, W.R., 1967, *Second thoughts*, London, Karnac.

26   James, D.C., 1994, 'Holding' & 'containing' in the group and society, in *The psyche and the social world*, eds Brown, D. & Zinkin, L., London, Routledge, pp. 60–79.

27   Piaget, J. & Cook, M., 1952, *The origin of intelligence in the child*, London, Routledge & Kegan Paul.

28   Through a psychological mechanism called projective identification, a primitive and powerful form of projection that expels the intolerable feeling.

29   Bion, op. cit.

30   Argyris, C., 1964, *Integrating the individual and the organization*, New York, Wiley, p. 4; Coutu, D., 2002, The anxiety of learning, the HBR interview, in *Harvard Business*

Review, March, pp. 2–8; Schein, E.H., 1989, Planned change theory, in McLennan, R., ed., *Managing organizational change*, London, Prentice Hall International; Schein, E.H., 1997, Empowerment, coercive persuasion and organizational learning: do they connect? *Henley Management College Working Paper 9718*, Henley, UK; Waldhoff, H.-P., 2007, Unthinking the closed personality: Norbert Elias, group analysis and unconscious processes in a research group, part II, in *Group Analysis*, *40*, 478–506.

31   Bion, op. cit.
32   Stern, D., 1985, *The interpersonal world of the infant*, New York, Basic Books.
33   Stern, op. cit.; Trevarthen, C., 1979, Communication and cooperation in early infancy: a description of primary intersubjectivity, in Bullowa, M., ed., 1979, *Before speech: the beginning of interpersonal communication*, Cambridge, Cambridge University Press.
34   Stern, op. cit.
35   This is no different to the process in a therapeutic group, though the focus and depth are different.
36   Hochschild, A., 1997, *The time bind*, New York, Henry Holt.
37   Foulkes, S.H. & Anthony, E.J., 1957, *Group psychotherapy: the psychoanalytic approach*, London, Karnac, p. 149.
38   Nitsun, M., 1996, *The anti group: destructive forces in the group and their creative potential*, London, Routledge, p. 123.
39   Thornton, op cit.
40   Stern, op. cit.
41   Dalal, F., 1998, *Taking the group seriously: towards a post-Foulkesian group analytic theory*, London, Routledge; Senge quotes Fred Kofman: (The self is) 'A point of view that unifies the flow of experience into a coherent narrative – a narrative striving to connect with other narratives', Senge, P., 1994, *The fifth discipline fieldbook*, London, Nicholas Brealey, p. 26.
42   Kets de Vries, M.F.R., 2005, Leadership group coaching in action: the Zen of creating high performance teams, in *Academy of Management Executive*, *19* (1), 61–76.
43   Trevarthen, op. cit.
44   Foulkes, S.H., 1990, *Selected papers of S. H. Foulkes: psychoanalysis and group analysis*, London, Karnac, p. 232.
45   Schein, op. cit.

Chapter 3: Looking deeper: the secret life of groups

46   Foulkes, S.H., 1973, The group as matrix of the individual's mental life, reproduced in Foulkes, 1990, op. cit.

47 Coined by Searles, H., 1962, The informational value of the supervisor's emotional experiences, in Searles, H., 1965, *Collected papers on schizophrenia and related subjects*, London, Hogarth.
48 Foulkes & Anthony, op. cit.
49 Stern, 1985, op. cit.
50 That is unwanted, 'forgotten'.
51 Foulkes, S.H., 1964, *Therapeutic group analysis*, London, George Allen & Unwin.
52 Foulkes & Anthony, op. cit.
53 Ramachandran, V.S., 2005, *A brief tour of human consciousness: from impostor poodles to purple numbers*, New York, Pi Press.
54 Kohut, H., 2001, *The analysis of the self*, p. 494; Trevarthen, C., 1977, Descriptive analyses of infant communicative behaviour, in H.R. Schaffer (ed.), *Studies in mother–infant interaction*, London, Academic Press.
55 Thornton, op. cit.
56 Foulkes & Anthony, op. cit., p. 152.
57 Ibid., p. 151.
58 Foulkes, 1964, op. cit.
59 Searles, H., op. cit.; Stimmel, B., 1995, Resistance to awareness of the supervisor's transferences with special reference to the parallel process, *International Journal of Psychoanalysis, 76*, 609–618; Wiener, J., 2007, The analyst's countertransference when supervising: friend or foe? *Journal of Analytical Psychology, 52* (1), 51–71.

Chapter 4: Eight group factors influencing learning and change

60 Thornton, C., 2008, *Practitioners mature in the group*, unpublished thesis, Manchester Metropolitan University, UK.
61 Yalom, I., 1995, *The theory and practice of group psychotherapy*, 4th ed., New York, Basic Books.
62 Gregory, C., Lockwood-Edwards, M. & Wright, J., 2008, *Action learning matters*, available to download from www.navca.org.uk
63 Kellerman, H. (ed.), 1981, *Group cohesion*, London, Grune and Stratton; Yalom, I., 1995, *The theory and practice of group psychotherapy*, 4th ed., New York, Basic Books.
64 Or 'attachment' in Bowlby's terms. Bowlby, J., 1969, *Attachment*, London, Hogarth Press.
65 Argyris, C., 1992, *On organizational learning*, Oxford, Blackwell, p. 422.
66 Yalom, op. cit.

67   Gregory et al., op. cit.
68   Lewin, K., 1952, *Field theory in social science*, London, Harper.

Chapter 5: Understanding organizations, groups and teams: systems thinking

69   Argyris & Schon, op. cit.
70   Von Bertalanffy, L., 1968, *General systems theory*, New York, Braziller.
71   Senge, op. cit.
72   Aronson, D., 2002, *How systems thinkers avoid common reasoning fallacies*, available at www.thinking.net
73   Senge, op. cit.
74   Morgan, G., 1996, *Images of organizations*, 2nd ed., Thousand Oaks, CA, Sage.
75   In this explanation, you could substitute the term 'subsystem' (to indicate that you see the team as part of a larger system) and the rest would remain unchanged.
76   Senge, op. cit., p. 69.
77   Bateson, op. cit.; Capra, op. cit.
78   Bohm, D., 1980, *Wholeness and the implicate order*, London, Routledge & Kegan Paul.
79   Morgan, op. cit.
80   Whyte, W.H., 1984, The gifted pedestrian, *Ekistics*, *306*, 224–230.
81   Surowiecki, J., 2005, *The wisdom of crowds*, London, Abacus.
82   Blackwell, D., 1998, Bounded instability, group analysis, and the matrix: organizations under stress, *Group Analysis*, *31*, 532.
83   Lewin, K., 1952, *Field theory in social science*, London, Harper.
84   Argyris, C., 1990, *Overcoming organizational defenses: facilitating organizational learning*, Boston, Allyn & Bacon.
85   Morgan, op. cit.
86   Bion, W.R., 1962, A theory of thinking, *International Journal of Psychoanalysis*, *43*, 306–310.
87   Morgan, op. cit.
88   Nicholas & Twaddell, op. cit., p. 18.
89   Surowiecki, op. cit.
90   Ibid., pp. 173–184.
91   Sayles, L.R. & Strauss, G., 1966, *Human behaviour in organizations*, London, Prentice Hall.
92   Janis, I., 1982, *Groupthink*, Boston, Houghton Mifflin.
93   Sunstein, C.R., 2003, *Why societies need dissent*, London, Harvard University Press.
94   Blomberg, S.B. & Harrington, J.E., 2000, A theory of rigid extremists and flexible moderates with an application to the U.S. Congress, *American Economic Review*, *90* (3), 605–620.

95   Maier, N. & Solem, A., 1952, The contribution of a discussion leader to the quality of group thinking: the effective use of minority opinions, *Human Relations*, *5*, 277–288.

96   Keyes, K., 1981, *The hundredth monkey*, Coos Bay, OR, Vision Books.

97   de Maré, P., Piper, R. & Thompson, S., 1991, *Koinonia: from hate, through dialogue, to culture in the large group*, New York, Karnac.

98   Mumby, T., 1975, Large groups in industry, in Kreeger, L., ed., *The large group*, London, Karnac.

99   Lawrence, W.G., 2005, *An introduction to social dreaming: transforming thinking*, London, Karnac.

100   www.theworldcafe.com

101   Harrison Owen, published at www.openspaceworld.com

Chapter 6: Team coaching

102   Nicholas & Twaddell, op. cit., p. 11.

103   Thompson L., 2000, *Making the team, a guide for managers*, Upper Saddle River, NJ, Prentice Hall, p. 2.

104   Kets de Vries, op. cit.

105   See www.myersbriggs.org

106   Tuckman, B.W., 1965, Developmental sequence in small groups, *Psychological Bulletin*, *63*, 384–399. See also www.infed.org/thinkers/tuckman.htm

107   Kubler-Ross, E., 1989, *On death and dying*, London, Routledge. Also run a web search for a range of versions and views. Helpful to treat the 'stages' as not necessarily wholly sequential, and acknowledge individual differences in response.

108   See 'Dealing with anger in a group', in Chapter 9, Senge, P., 1994, *The fifth discipline fieldbook*, London, Nicholas Brealey.

109   Karpman, S., 1968, Fairy tales and script drama analysis, *Transactional Analysis Bulletin*, *7* (26), 39–43, which can be downloaded free at www.karpmandramatriangle.com/articles.html Also known as the rescue triangle.

110   www.belbin.com See also Belbin, 2008, *The Belbin guide to succeeding at work*, Cambridge, Belbin.

111   Hersey, P., Blanchard, K.H. & Johnson, D.E., 2001, *Management of organizational behavior*, Englewood Cliffs, NJ, Prentice Hall.

112   See http://en.wikipedia.org/wiki/Ishikawa_diagram

113   See http://en.wikipedia.org/wiki/Mind_map

114   See http://en.wikipedia.org/wiki/SWOT_analysis

115   See www.businessballs.com/pestanalysisfreetemplate.htm

116   Austen, J., 1816, *Emma*, London, Pan edition 1972, p. 365.
117   Argyris, 1990, op. cit., p. 50.
118   Grenny, J., July 2009, information at www.vitalsmarts.com

Chapter 7: Learning group coaching

119   The journal *Action Learning: Research and Practice* is a good starting point.
120   Pedler, M., Burgoyne, J. & Brook, C., 2005, What has action learning learned to become?, *Action Learning*, *2* (1), 49–68.
121   See note 1.
122   Thornton, 2008, op. cit.
123   Senge, P., 1990, *The fifth discipline*, London, Century Business.
124   What is an organization that it may learn? In Argyris & Schon, op. cit.
125   Thornton, 2008, op. cit.

Chapter 8: Supervision groups

126   Bernard, J.M. & Goodyear, R.K., 2009, Fundamentals of clinical supervision, London; Carroll, M., 1996, *Counselling supervision: theory, skills & practice*, London, Sage; Hawkins, P. & Shohet, R., 2000, *Supervision in the helping professions*, 2nd ed., Oxford, Oxford University Press; Hawkins, P. & Smith, N., 2006, *Coaching, mentoring and organizational consultancy*, London, McGraw-Hill.
127   Hawkins & Shohet, op. cit.
128   Bernard & Goodyear, op. cit.
129   Wiener, J., Mizen, R. & Duckham, J., 2003, *Supervising and being supervised: a practice in search of a theory*, New York, Palgrave Macmillan.
130   Bernard & Goodyear, op. cit.
131   Searles, 1962, op. cit.
132   Driver, C. & Martin, E., 2002, *Supervising psychotherapy: psychoanalytic and psychodynamic perspectives*, London, Sage; Driver, C. & Martin, E., 2005, *Supervision and the analytic attitude*, London, Whurr; Petts, A. & Shapley, B., 2007, On supervision: psychoanalytic and Jungian analytic perspectives, London, Karnac; Wiener et al., op. cit.
133   Carroll, op. cit., p. 133.
134   Banks, M., The transition from therapist to supervisor; Driver, C., Internal states in the supervisory relationship; Stewart, J., The container and the contained, all in Driver

& Martin, 2002, op. cit.; Howard, S., Models of supervision, in Petts & Shapley, op. cit.; Thomas, M., Through the looking glass: creativity in supervision, in Driver & Martin, 2005, op. cit.

135 Moss, E., 1995, Group supervision: focus on counter-transference, *International Journal of Group Psychotherapy*, *45* (4), 537–548.

136 Yorke, V., 2005, Bion's vertex as a supervisory object, in Driver & Martin, 2005, op. cit.

137 Carroll, op. cit.

138 Hawkins & Shohet, op. cit.

139 Searles, 1962, op. cit.

140 Fuller, V.G., 2003, Supervision in groups, in Wiener et al., op. cit.

141 Summarized from Perry, C., 2003, Into the labyrinth: a developing approach to supervision, in Wiener et al., op. cit.

142 Stimmel, B., 1995, Resistance to awareness of the supervisor's transferences with special reference to the parallel process, *International Journal of Psychoanalysis*, *76*, 609–618.

143 Berman, A. & Berger, M., 2007, Matrix and reverie in supervision groups, in *Group Analysis*, *40* (2), 236–250.

144 Casement, P., 1985, *On learning from the patient*, London, Routledge.

145 Sharpe, M. & Blackwell, D., 1987, Creative supervision through student involvement, *Group Analysis*, *20* (3), 195–208.

146 Moss, op. cit., p. 547.

147 Bernard & Goodyear, op. cit.

148 Ibid.

149 Zinkin, L., 1988, Supervision: the impossible profession. In Kugler, P. (ed.), *Jungian perspectives on clinical supervision*, Einsiedeln, Switzerland, Daimon Verlag.

150 Yorke, V., 2005, Bion's vertex as a supervisory object, in Driver & Martin, 2005, op. cit.

151 The lists in the boxes are based on Meg Sharpe's classifications in Presenting groups effectively, in Sharpe, M. (ed.), 1995, *The third eye: supervision of analytic groups*, London, Routledge.

Chapter 9: Strategies for tackling problem behaviour

152 Senge, op. cit.

153 Tuckman, B.W., 1965, Developmental sequence in small groups, *Psychological Bulletin*, *63*, 384–399.

154 Marquardt (Marquardt, M.J., 2004, *Optimizing the power of action learning: solving problems and building leaders in real*

time, Palo Alto, CA, Davies-Black) claims that a coach can avert the need for an action learning set's 'storming' stage. I think this is wishful thinking, but I wonder whether the questioning process, by ritualizing conflict, paradoxically reduces threat and tension.

155   Yalom, op. cit.
156   Berne, E., 1961, *Games people play*, London, Penguin.

Chapter 10: Groups that do not work: understanding and tackling dysfunctional patterns in group behaviour

157   Bion, W.R., 1961, *Experiences in groups*, London, Routledge.
158   Karpman, S., 1968, Fairy tales and script drama analysis, *Transactional Analysis Bulletin*, *7* (26), 39–43.
159   Argyris, C., 1995, Action science and organizational learning, *Journal of Managerial Psychology*, *10* (6), 20–26.
160   His theory extends an understanding of individual and interpersonal resistance to change with resistance to change at the organizational level.
161   Argyris, 1990, op. cit., p. 27.
162   Argyris, 1992, op. cit., p. 105.
163   Argyris & Schon, 1996, op. cit.
164   Bateson, op. cit.
165   Argyris, 1995, op. cit.
166   This relates to overcoming obstacles to learning, as described in 'The development of thinking and obstacles to learning' in Chapter 2.
167   Argyris, 1992, op. cit.

Chapter 11: Managing beginnings, middles and endings: boundaries of the group

168   This obvious truth can feel much less obvious when working with a group who wish to make it your responsibility.
169   Palshaugen, O., 2001, The use of words, in Reason, P. & Bradbury, H. (eds), *Handbook of action research*, London, Sage.
170   Kolb, D.A., Rubin, I.M. & Osland, J., 1991, *Organizational behavior: an experiential approach*, Englewood Cliffs, NJ, Prentice Hall.

absence 216–17, 236

acceptance 29, 35, 37, 40–2, 53, 67, 83, 212, 224–5

action learning 34, 41, 54, 66, 77, 108, 148–56, 167, 199, 216; as a tool in culture change 67–8, 98, 156; compared to Balint groups 156–9; conventionalised exchange in 41; gains from 155–6, 163; origins and development of 149–50; protocols 154–5; set 9, 12, 34, 37; what happens in a set 151; what is 149; structure of 152–3

admiration 54, 72–4, 102, 169

amplification of feelings 35, 171: *see also* feelings

anger 35, 62, 68, 136, 138, 139–40, 175, 218–21, 226; dealing with overt in a group 197–204; *see also* hostility

antiquity of groups 24

anxiety 37–8, 82–3, 96, 106, 109, 126–7, 129, 144, 175–6, 186, 206, 215–16, 219, 238, 240; of coach 125, 129, 139–40, 163, 177, 180–1, 184–5, 240; *see also* panic and helplessness

Argyris, C. 31, 104–5, 119, 142, 214, 228–31

authority 81–2, 104, 148, 183, 186, 197, 201

awaydays 122–4

Balint groups 12, 156–9, 167, 199

barriers, interpersonal 70, 81, 120, 145, 236

basic assumptions 219–24

beginnings 34, 36, 52, 189, 195, 233–4, 238–40

belonging 42, 66–70, 74, 98–9, 183

Berne, E. 210

Bion, W.R. 30, 102, 107, 219–21

boredom 49, 139, 210, 218, 238

boundary: and holding 33–4, 243; keeper 81–2, 240; of coaching relationship 55, 177; of group 81–2, 188; of group coaching 8, 183, 233–249; of system 93–4; of team 12, 93, 137; of time, *see* time, boundary of

capacity to hold a group, developing 33

change 3, 5, 15, 21, 24, 32, 39, 43, 48, 55, 65, 74–5, 77, 81, 156, 168; in organizations x–xii, 13, 35, 67–8, 78–9, 87, 89, 92–3, 95–8, 105, 107, 123, 126–8, 130–3, 143–4, 156, 222–7, 229–32, 241–2, 248

collaborate, capacity to 4, 7, 16, 61, 73–4, 101, 119, 121–2, 125–6, 127, 135, 166–7, 193–7, 214–232, 242

communication 46–52, 79, 96, 119, 124, 127, 130, 145, 172, 174, 182, 208, 246; amplification in groups 25, 35, 43, 62–3, 171, 221; and performance 42, 100–1, 105, 120, 123, 130, 135–6, 143–4, 194, 230–1; barriers to 24, 61, 69, 100–1, 108 9, 145, 208, 236; coach's role in 38, 47, 82, 100, 121, 167–8; group concept of 48–52, 96, 106, 145, 182,

228; non-verbal 10, 25, 41, 50, 52, 140–1, 159, 171, 188, 209, 217–18; patterns of 11, 48, 119, 143; technology 13, 145, 160

competition 12, 72–4, 77, 102–3, 109, 137–8, 168–9, 179, 181, 195

complexity, working with 89, 92–100, 118, 167, 174

condenser phenomena 58–9

confidentiality 136, 162, 178

conflict 102–3, 108–9, 113, 127–8, 135, 197–204, 209–10, 216, 221–8, 238

conflicting messages 78, 97, 135, 139–44, 227–32

connectedness 4, 17, 66–70

containing 28, 33–4, 106, 126, 185

continuous professional development 83, 108, 141, 255–7

courage 51, 66, 68, 70, 75–6, 209

CPD see continuous professional development

crying 34, 204–6, 212–3 see also distress

culture change 13, 67–8, 78–9, 98, 105–9, 130–3, 143, 148, 156, 186, 222–4

de Maré, P. 107–8

decision-making 89, 103–5, 113, 120, 170–1, 195–7, 220–1

destructive behaviour 55, 61, 81–2, 106–7, 204

destructive experiences 45, 62, 72, 204

dialogue 76, 96, 106–9, 119, 127, 195–7, 250

distress 175–6, 204–6, see also crying

diversity 12, 15–16, 103–5, 113, 148, 168, 185, 188

dominating behaviour, dealing with 206–8, 210

drama triangle 127, 223–7

early departers 246–7

emulation 74–5

encouragement 77–9; coach's use of 6, 11, 32, 35, 38, 48, 58, 73–4, 96–8,
153, 176–7, 183–4, 187, 195–6, 200–1, 204–5, 207, 211, 218, 227, 230, 238, 240, 246–7, 250

endings 10, 234, 238–9, 243–9; psychological dimensions of 244–5; unconscious feelings about 202–4; 244–7; see also early departers

environment: business 6, 16, 90, 120, 124, 128, 137–8, 142, 211; group 148, 233–6; holding 28

envy 61, 70, 72–4, 77

exchange 7, 9, 24, 29–30, 32, 39–43, 52, 56–7, 70, 84, 135, 153; as the medium of culture 96, 106; conventionalized in action learning sets and team coaching 41–2

expectations 178, 215, 222; conflicting 97, 123, 139–43; unspoken or unconscious 33, 107, 118, 139–41

fear 25, 61–2, 104, 106–9, 138, 167, 169–70, 175, 183, 186, 199–200, 209, 219, 230

feelings: and action 38; apposite and inappropriate 27; containing difficult feelings 33–6, 62, 138, 193–213, 244–6; contradictory 78–9, 140–2; expression of 38, 61, 71, 133, 139, 153, 158, 179, 195, 201, 239–40, 246; how we understand others' 25, 53; positive xii, 4, 25, 53, 68, 133, 184, 221; reflection process and 62, 170–1, 175; strong 27, 54, 68, 83, 106; transferential 54; use of coach's 38, 83, 140–2, 188, 245, 247; unwanted 60, 69, 71, 229; see also acceptance, amplification of feelings, anger, anxiety, competition, destructive behavior, destructive feelings, distress, fear, frustration, hostility, loss, panic and helplessness, relief, sadness, security, shame

Foulkes, S.H. 46, 49, 255–6

frustration 28, 30, 35, 51, 63, 67–8, 75, 78–9, 107, 139–40, 143, 171, 175–6, 179, 210, 218, 230, 238

goals 16, 46, 195, 215; and reality 35, 97, 119, 123, 135, 222, 224, 227–8; clarifying 129–35, 145–6, 218, 232, 240; conflicting 140; driven 117, 126; learning 7, 11, 148, 162, 177; of team coaching 81, 118–22, 127, 129–30, 144, 218, 227–8, 244; shared 6, 11–12, 100–1, 102–3, 122, 126, 148, 155–6; *see also* objectives
Goleman, D. 4, 25
good intentions 108, 123, 241–2
group analysis xi, 15–16, 46, 165
group coach 5–6, 12–13, 26, 65, 67–8, 73–4, 76, 148, 152, 154, 220–1; characteristics of 51, 83; role of 28, 32, 36–9, 45, 48–9, 51–2, 58, 61–2, 66, 68, 74, 77, 80–83, 87, 90, 98, 105, 114, 144, 186, 206, 209, 211–12, 217, 234–5, 237–8
group coaching: advantages of 6–7, 25, 70, 78, 96, 105, 121, 144; beginning 34, 36, 52, 177, 195, 238–40; ending 238–9, 243–9; final session of 247–9; middle 238–43; standards 8–9; telephone 9–10, 144–5, 159–61; what is 5, 9–11, 80, 218, 228
group dynamics ix, 8–9, 45, 84, 88, 140–1, 165, 183, 203–4; *see also* group matrix
group matrix 47–49
group performance coaching 79–80
group, physical environment of 235–6
group principles, underlying 5–6, 44–65
group processes, nine 44–65
group sessions, beginnings, middles and endings 238–9
group supervision 165–8; advantages and limitations 168; beginning 177–80; complexity of dynamic 167, 172–4; holding in 167; key factors 185–6; learning 166–8; managing rivalry and competition in 169; reflection process in 170–7; structuring 178–80; theory 165
group task 38, 46–7, 183
group, time and the 234–5
groups: and teams 11–13; anxiety in

215–6, *see also* anxiety; boredom in, *see* boredom; disengaged 49, 218; dysfunction 70, 214–232; large 4, 7, 9–10, 105–13; new 34, 36, 52, 189, 195, 238–240; setting up, *see* group, new

holding 24, 28–30; a group 33–4, 38–9; and exchange in groups 32; as time goes on 36–8; difficult feelings 34–6
Hochschild, A. 36
hostility 62, 70, 108–9, 127–8, 221–4

idealization 68–9, 74–5
implicit knowing 25, 41, 50–1, 205; *see also* non-conscious
interpersonal learning 15, 25, 70–1, 144; *see also* learning
isomorphism, *see* reflection process

Kolb, D. 242–3

large group, restructuring into smaller groups 109–13
large groups: *see* group, large
lateness 189, 216–7
learning 6–12, 23–43, 45, 49, 62–3, 65–81, 88, 98, 111, 123, 143–4, 181–2, 193, 199, 205, 223, 229, 239, 246–7, 250; barriers to 28, 30–1, 54–56, 142–3, 166–7, 219, 229–31, *see also* Bion, Argyris; grounded in emotional relationship 31–2; interpersonal, *see* interpersonal learning; Kolb cycle and 242–3; multi-sensory 31–2; styles 166, 188, 243; transfer of 240–3
learning group 5, 11–12, 147–63, 166, 168, 177, 179, 205, 207, 237, 244, 247; interpersonal skill gains in 155–6, 163
learning, social 109; *see also* social intelligence
location 59–62, 225, 227
loss 37–8, 204, 227, 243–7; of face 7, 185

management development programmes 11, 155, 162–3
middles 238–43

mirroring 27, 46, 52–6, 62, 68, 76, 93, 102–3, 139–42, 166, 171, 175; negative, *see* negative mirroring

negative mirroring 54–6
non-conscious 42, 48, 52, 72, 75, 77, 129, 145, 159, 194, 234, 246; *see also* implicit knowing
normalizing 73–4, 99, 168, 199, 216
note-taking 111, 187–9

objectives 9–11, 123, 126, 130–3, 135, 151, 197, 222–7; *see also* goals
open space technology (OST) 111–3
organizational defences 142, 228–31

panic and helplessness 35, 99, 170–1, 181, 185, 212–13, 226; *see also* anxiety
paradox 29–30, 32, 42, 49, 69, 79, 100, 208, 210–11, 222, 228, 230, 232, 241–2;
necessity of 96–8
parallel process: *see* reflection process
process breaks 194, 201
projection 25–7, 33, 52–4, 83–4, 183

reality check 25
reflection process 49, 62–3, 151, 165, 168, 170–7
relief 59, 62, 70, 78–9, 139–40, 202–4, 219, 221, 244, 248
repetition 27, 29, 40
resonance 57–9, 68, 189
Revans R. 149–50

sadness 248
scapegoating 60–1, 69, 81–2, 219
security 25, 28–30, 33–34, 37, 42, 45, 60–2, 177, 184, 249
self-organizing processes 95, 109–13
shame 56, 167
silence 36, 57, 78–9, 158–9, 180–1, 185, 198, 208–10, 216
skilful discussion 6, 195–7
Stern, D. 25
supervision: *see* group supervision
supervision group: *see* group supervision

supervision of groups, reflection process in 170–7
supervision group theory 165
supervisor, common errors 180–5
system administration 81–2, 233–7; getting the conditions right 234
system boundaries 93–4
system, working with more than one part of the 100–3
systems theory 15–17, 69, 79, 88–100; *see also* systems thinking
systems thinking 85–114; systems thinking and teams 119, 137, 144; *see also* systems theory

team coach 15, 55, 93, 101, 119, 137–9, 148; characteristics of 51, 83–4, 118; *see also* group coach and group coach, role of
team coaching 5, 7, 71, 117–46, 166, 175–6, 211–13, 231, 241–2, 244; advantages of 105, 120–2, 231; beginning 34, 36, 52, 177, 195, 238–240; client relationship risks in 134–5;contracting process 129–34; conventionalized exchange in 41–2; creating opportunities for 122–4; ending 238–9, 243–9; goals of 119–20, 130, 135, 141–3; importance of timing in 143–4; interviewing individual members 135–6; middle 238–43; using tools and models 124–9; virtual teams 144–5; what is 9–13, 122; working with more than one team 100–3;
team, dysfunctional 214–32
team leader 71, 92, 134, 136–9
team tools 124–9
team, what is a? 11–13, 90–3, 118–19
team, when is a group a? 11–13
telephone group coaching *see* group coaching, telephone
therapy 13, 36, 46, 66, 165, 177, 182–3
thinking, development of 30–1
time: and the group 40–2, 48; as a key component of coaching and learning 4, 8–11, 29, 32, 34–5, 52, 54, 75–6, 122, 153, 155–6, 160, 197, 231; time boundaries 42, 81,

179–80, 184, 199, 216–17, 233–249;
coach's use of 38, 81, 96, 150, 169,
234–5, 241; in system thinking 89,
93, 96; paced for learning 150, 152,
163, 197, 207, 234, 241, 247; poverty
36, 159
tools: in team coaching 124–9;
common mistakes in using 125–6
transfer of learning 123, 240–3
transference 26–8, 52, 54–5, 189, 228
translation 52

uncertainty 7, 12–13, 119, 125, 154,
155–6, 181, 197

unconscious 26, 37, 48, 52, 55–8, 60,
70, 72, 108, 135, 140–3, 168, 169,
171–2, 174, 176, 219–32
unspoken conflicts 139–43,
219–32

vignettes 17
virtual teams 144–5

Winnicott, D.W. 28
witnessing 66, 75–77, 209
world café 109–11

yes but 54, 210